RE-IMAGINING THERAPY

DATE DUE

APR 2 1 2002	

INQUIRIES IN SOCIAL CONSTRUCTION

Series editors
Kenneth J. Gergen and John Shotter

Inquiries in Social Construction is designed to facilitate across disciplinary and national boundaries, a revolutionary dialogue within the social sciences and humanities. Central to this dialogue is the idea that all presumptions of the real and the good are constructed within relations among people. This dialogue gives voice to a new range of topics, including the social construction of the person, rhetoric and narrative in the construction of reality, the role of power in making meanings, postmodernist culture and thought, discursive practices, the social constitution of the mental, dialogic process, reflexivity in theory and method, and many more. The series explores the problems and prospects generated by this new relational consciousness, and its implications for science and social life.

Also in this series

Discursive Psychology
Derek Edwards and Jonathan Potter

Therapy as Social Construction
edited by Sheila McNamee and Kenneth J. Gergen

Psychology and Postmodernism
edited by Steinar Kvale

Constructing the Social
edited by Theodore R. Sarbin and John I. Kitsuse

Conversational Realities
John Shotter

Power/Gender
edited by H. Lorraine Radtke and Henderikus J. Stam

After Postmodernism
edited by Herbert W. Simons and Michael Billig

The Social Self
edited by David Bakhurst and Christine Sypnowich

RE-IMAGINING THERAPY

Living Conversations and Relational Knowing

EERO RIIKONEN AND
GREGORY MADAN SMITH

SAGE Publications
London • Thousand Oaks • New Delhi

SAGE Publications Ltd
6 Bonhill Street
London EC2A 4PU

SAGE Publications Inc.
2455 Teller Road
Thousand Oaks, California 91320

SAGE Publications India Pvt Ltd
32, M-Block Market
Greater Kailash – I
New Delhi 110 048

British Library Cataloguing in Publication data

A catalogue record for this book is available
from the British Library.

ISBN 0 8039 7653 4
ISBN 0 8039 7654 2 (pbk)

Library of Congress catalog record available

Typeset by Mayhew Typesetting, Rhayader, Powys
Printed in Great Britain by Biddles Ltd, Guildford, Surrey

Contents

Foreword

Kenneth J. Gergen and Sheila McNamee

For the therapeutic community language has always had a fascination, but only in a secondary sense. That is, language furnished the pieces to a puzzle about a world that lay outside language itself. With intense concentration on language, the therapist might hope to gain insight into the complex dynamics of the psyche, into unconscious forces, hidden memories, cognitive structures, and the like. Or, by examining patterns of language within families, the therapist might lay bare the structures of family relationships, or self-sustaining and self-defeating logics. In a broad sense, the prevailing orientation toward language was *structuralist*: language served as an expression or manifestation of an otherwise hidden structure that was elsewhere than language itself. The reasons are many, but structuralism is now in recession. With the growing interest in social construction, narratives, metaphors, and the co-construction of meaning within the therapeutic community, we move into the domain of *post-structuralism*. In this case we find that language is no longer an expression or manifestation of something else, but gains importance in itself. In the post-structuralist frame, language essentially constitutes the psyche, the family, the pathology, and the remaining family of therapeutic objects. The person is only such by virtue of the ways in which he/she participates in or is situated by language: families are what they are by virtue of their forms of communication; pathology is constituted in and through language. The present offering by Riikonen and Smith significantly extends the post-structuralist dialogues.

In this sense, the volume is an entry into conversations carried on in a wide range of important predecessors, including M. White and D. Epston's *Narrative Means to Therapeutic Ends* (1990), D. Spence's *Narrative Truth and Historical Truth* (1982), S. Friedman's edited book *The New Language of Change* (1993), S. De Shazer's *Words Were Originally Magic* (1994), J. Freedman and G. Combs' *Narrative Therapy* (1995), H.J.M. Hermans and E. Hermans-Jansen's *Self Narratives* (1995), H. Rosen and K.T. Kuehlwein's *Constructing Realities* (1996), and our own edited compilation, *Therapy as Social Construction* (1993), along with K.J. Gergen's *Realities and Relationships* (1994). However, Riikonen and Smith extend these conversations in very important ways. At the outset, they inject into the literature a much needed emphasis on the pragmatic features of language, the capacity of words (as forms of action) to achieve consequences both in therapy and daily life. Language by their account is not a reflection of another world, but an implement of construction for the world we now occupy. Closely related, the action consequences of words are tied intimately to relationships, to the dialogic give and take of human interchange. We don't find here, for example, a client's disembodied narrative cut away from their function in relationships, but an emphasis on continuous, momentary and participatory movements in sense-making. And within this context the authors grapple as well with issues of power and politics in therapy, not with a one-dimensional claim to righteousness but within a complex conversation without close.

Yet, there are two additional features of this work that are striking in their originality. The first is the introduction into the therapeutic conversation of what we may characterize as a Dionysian element. Why, they ask, must the therapeutic process be so heavily freighted with images of disease and cure, seriousness and sadness, fear and turmoil? Why must there be such a strong emphasis on the concrete and the real? After all, there is nothing about the nature of human suffering that demands these as therapeutic responses. So we find the present work surging with spontaneity and joy, playing hide and seek with metaphors, and inviting readers to share in the mirth. There is more to the Dionysian metaphor, for after all, Dionysus was a god. And in the present text we find, faintly present on the borders of 'the game,' an abiding consciousness of profundity, the sense that the therapeutic process in its ideal form, may be linked with an awesome and infinite power.

Finally, and most importantly, the present work opens a new and exciting vista for deliberation on the therapeutic process. Fully aware of their post-structural posture, and the inability of scholarly words to 'capture' the world it pretends to portray, Riikonen and Smith chart a new territory of expression. We may characterize the text as 'performative,' in its specific attempt to *perform* as opposed to *reflect* its subject matter. The authors do not wish so much to describe optimal therapy as to demonstrate its potentials within the text itself. The text moves, then, not with an ineluctable logic in a predetermined direction, but with aleatory verve. With robust and startling juxtapositions we move in and out of various conversations, monologues, and imaginings. We are exposed as well to multiple voices, some fictitious and others scholarly, some self doubting and others authoritative, some doing street talk and others poetry . . . and sometimes the various voices are blended. As readers, we are invited, then, to take advantage of our own multiplicity, our capacities for spontaneous creativity, and our deep embeddedness in the hurly-burly of conversational movement, and to share these with others – including the therapeutic client. It is a work in the service of joy, and we are pleased to lend our applause.

A good book is written with the purpose that after reading it the reader knows significantly less about many things. (Anonymous)

Preface

There are many people without whom this book would never have come into being, and several whose contributions to the text have been invaluable. The contributions of two of these have consisted of long-standing support, countless discussions of a wide variety of topics related to the themes and a lovingly critical attitude. These two are the authors' wives, Sara Vataja and Jane Tiggeman, themselves both prominent in the field of therapy. Also important has been Juho, the now 6-year-old son of Eero Riikonen and Sara Vataja: it would be hard to find a better person to teach in practice what this book preaches.

For Eero Riikonen, a constant additional source of inspiration has been close friend and colleague Mikko Makkonen. His ideas and visions have been both a catalyst and a source material for creative fermentation. Many themes and viewpoints simply would not exist without him, and in some places it is impossible to draw a line between his ideas or words and ours. It would be fair to have an acknowledgement to him on many of the pages. For Gregory Smith, a particular recognition must go to David Glazbrook, for his support and many conversations filled with the lightness and depth we try to describe in the book.

Other people who have had significant effects on the direction and results of the writing process are: our respective closest colleagues in Finland and in Australia (Michael and Cheryl White), Mark Beyebach (the future novelist) from Salamanca, Robyn Penman from Canberra, John Shotter from University of New Hampshire, Kenneth Gergen from Swarthmore College, Ben Furman and Tapani Ahola from

Helsinki, Michael Hjerth from Uppsala, Steve De Shazer and Insoo Kim Berg.

Without the creative minds and warm hearts of our clients and trainees, and without the support of the Rehabilitation Foundation in Helsinki, the task would have been impossible. The research director of Rehabilitation Foundation, Aila Järvikoski, and the managing director of the same organization, Ilpo Vilkkumaa, deserve the highest praise for their open-mindedness and positive attitude towards the project. Eero Riikonen wants to thank the National Research and Development Centre for Welfare and Health (STAKES), which has consistently supported the project, and thanks must also go to Jacky Morris, Loretta Perry and Ian Law in Adelaide for comments and encouragement with earlier drafts.

Finally, special thanks are due to the wider families of both authors. Their dogged belief that our efforts were worthwhile has been a constant positive force for many years.

E.R.
G.S.

1
Orientations

Orientation 1: The gifts of words

She went by the name of Belisa Crepusculario, not because she had been baptised with that name or given it by her mother, but because she herself had searched until she found the poetry of 'beauty' and 'twilight' and cloaked herself in it. She made her living selling words. She journeyed through the country from the high cold mountains to the burning coasts, stopping at fairs and in markets where she set up four poles covered by a canvas awning under which she took refuge from the sun and rain to minister to her customers . . . Her prices were fair. For five centavos she delivered verses from memory; for seven she improved the quality of dreams; for nine she wrote love letters; for twelve she invented insults for irreconcilable enemies . . . To anyone who paid her fifty centavos in trade, she gave the gift of a secret word to drive away melancholy. It was not the same word for everyone, naturally, because that would have been collective deceit. Each person received his or her own word, with the assurance that no-one else would use it that way in this universe or beyond. (Isabel Allende, *The Stories of Eva Luna*, 1991: 5)

Orientation 2: Providential dialogues

This book is about different understandings of therapeutic practices – and different relationships to therapy. We have wanted to question taken-for-granted assumptions and to propose others which we feel are more promising.

The starting point is the obvious fact that therapy is conversation, or at least takes place in conversation, that is, with two or more people talking. The book is informed by many recent developments in post-modern and social constructionist thought. It is radically at odds with those traditional approaches to therapy which tend not to be interested in the conversation itself, and focus mainly on the 'information' gathered or the 'interventions' performed.

In starting the project our main interests were clear. We wanted to look closely at what actually happens in conversation and see if we could thus produce new ideas about how to develop practices and theories of helping. In doing this we set out to draw particularly upon social constructionist views, Mikhail Bakhtin's ideas about dialogue, and Ludwig Wittgenstein's ideas of language, particularly to look at language-in-the-speaking as opposed to texts, theories or abstractions of language (Shotter, 1993a,b; Wittgenstein, 1953: §§ 130, 132). We also wanted to connect some recent discussions of the therapy world to wider issues and dialogues. Moreover, it seemed to us that the perspectives and ideas we talked about could be applied to much more general issues regarding interaction, service cultures and even basic human rights.

It is well known that there exists an abundance of different approaches to therapy and counselling, each making claims regarding the specificity of its methods and its effectiveness in achieving results. Because the creation of distinctive packages of practices makes economic sense, there has so far been relatively little interest among therapists themselves in examining things like common elements or shared backgrounds. The interest in the study of commonalities is, however, steadily increasing.

A great number of psychotherapy outcome studies have shown that the results of therapies mostly correlate with the quality of the interpersonal relationship (measured by factors like 'warmth of the therapist', 'trust', 'experienced hope', 'constructiveness of conversation', 'feeling understood' etc.), not with factors like the methods used, or the length of training of the professionals involved. The so-called 'non-specific factors' have generally proved to be more important than the 'specific factors' (which supposedly relate to particular methods targeted at defined 'symptoms' or 'structures of personality').

There are many kinds of conceptual elements which different approaches to therapy share, mostly without notic-ing this sharing. They often tend, for example, to orientate in rather similar ways to questions about the nature of people, social interaction, problems/solutions and language. Many of them are informed by shared values or basic metaphors of which the representatives of the schools are not consciously aware or which they do not make explicit. *universals*

We have focused our attention on <u>domains of enquiry</u> and <u>conceptual resources</u> which we think are (or could be) of interest to *all* approaches to therapy and counselling. A main focus is on the relationship between metaphorical understanding and something we call good or <u>providential interaction</u>.

We believe that some of the ideas and principles illumi-nated in the text can indeed lead to the development of new practices. However, it is quite evident that more often we are just describing things that people, not only therapists but all of us, 'know very well in practice but not at all in theory'. We thus often highlight ways of talking which seem to be both helpful and common, but which to our knowl-edge are very seldom explicitly discussed. To do this is important, because their lack of inclusion means that these practices are often devalued. Often therapists practise in particular ways *despite* their models, rather than because of them, and if helpful practices are made visible, we believe they can be used more consciously and regularly.

We have tried to avoid looking at therapy through indi-vidualistic lenses. We try to describe, use and develop relational perspectives and metaphors (see Gergen, 1994; Shotter, 1993a,b). In accordance with these views, we see words primarily as tools, gestures and actions, not as labels for objective things. Indeed throughout the text we use the word 'word' loosely, inexactly, half-metaphorically, in a Bakhtinian vein. It refers to 'things people say' sometimes also to utterances and even gestures.

Examining Mikhail Bakhtin's ideas about dialogue and dialogical understanding (see Bakhtin, 1981; Shotter, 1993a; Wertsch, 1991) made us convinced that the world of therapy could indeed benefit from looking more closely at how we relate *to* and *with* language. Studying Bakhtin makes it also apparent that the relationship of words and social interaction is reflexive. Different ways of talking support different kinds of relationships and experiences – different experiences and relationships support different kinds of talking.

Both Shotter and Bakhtin make it clear that all knowledge of relationships cannot be given a descriptive form. We follow Shotter when he claims that relationships between people base themselves mostly on a special kind of knowledge – he calls it 'knowledge of the third kind'. It is not knowing 'what' (descriptive, theoretical) or 'how' (methodological), but 'knowing from' (a social situation). This type of knowledge has to do with how we relate to our situation or circumstances. It is anticipatory, participatory and practical (not external, disciplined, systematic or referential). It is closely connected to emotions and to the invitations we implicitly feel in interactions. And it has its appearance only in moments of interaction. It is thus something people constantly need in order to get along with other people (see Wittgenstein, 1953: § 154). Understanding 'knowledge' in these ways allows new possibilities for understanding therapy.

The concept of metaphor is central for our text. First, we have taken Wittgenstein's view of methods of (philosophical) research quite seriously and applied it to our own thinking and writing. Like him, we see the main task of research as being to find images and metaphors which, first, arrest the normal flow of automatic happenings, thoughts and actions to make taken-for-granted metaphors more obvious, and secondly, make new connections, possibilities or more productive metaphors visible (Shotter, 1993a: 81; Wittgenstein, 1953: §§ 130, 132).

Secondly, for us therapy is indeed largely about new connections and distinctions becoming visible through dialogue.

It thus is also about finding new ways of relating. These 'new ways' of relating may refer to the relationship to the 'problem', but also to life, to experience, to other people – or to oneself. These processes link with the metaphors through which we understand the relationship. Metaphors are explored and introduced through dialogue – not in some abstracted fashion.

The third point is the most difficult to formulate. It has to do with the fact that therapy is not an individual matter. It is not only about seeing new connections but also about creating *shared* visibilities, about promise seen *together* and about *connectedness*. We see therapy as a continuous development and reshaping of shared, providential (promising, inspiring) realities. These realities are clearly not attributes of individuals: they are not *in* people, but are rather something people themselves *are in*, and to which they act and react. They are genuinely dialogical phenomena produced jointly by the participants, and yet which cannot be totally controlled by them – joint action is more than the sum of its parts (see Shotter, 1993a). We claim throughout the book that 'metaphorical languages' are, because of their close connections to basic forms of sociality and to emotions, very important in the joint creation of these kinds of realities.

The dialogical approach we are proposing starts from the premiss that both helpful and problematic realities ('solutions' and 'problems') are examples of joint action in Shotter's sense. In line with this, we believe that psychotherapy is a manner of being and interacting with people, not a form of science. To practise this art we need a multitude of ways of co-creating contexts which allow for new relationships, movement and promise.

We see that our task is to re-imagine therapy: to see it in imaginative ways, to re-equip it with imagination, to 're-metaphoricize' it. This task is not made easier by various existing attempts to create systematic, detached and over-arching conceptualizations of therapeutic interaction. These forces are often unquestioned, so it is worth elaborating on the assumption of systematic understanding (see Johnson,

1993). In most theoretical disciplines there is an implicit metaphor that we should have a systematic 'overview' of the 'field' of knowledge. In these fields, we attempt to 'rise above' the 'field' to gain an 'overview' so that we can consistently follow all 'paths' of thought and can 'see' 'beyond' any 'blocks' or 'obstructions' which may arise to that 'path' of thought. The 'field' is consistent and uninterrupted, and everything can be 'seen' to 'proceed out' from a 'central position'. Anything which 'blocks' or 'stands in the way of' this 'movement out' from the 'central' premiss must be 'overcome' for the theory to 'guide' or 'direct' our understanding or action. In the field of therapy there is a range of theories about the nature of the person, how to categorize people or interaction patterns, how to form interventions, and so on. Each of these presents a systematic understanding of the person and processes of change.

These latter kinds of attempts can be seen even within accounts inspired by social constructionism: it is not uncommon to hear a lot of monological talk about multiple voices and serious and truth-exuding accounts of the need to avoid overarching truths. This is understandable to some extent. Many forces, some of them unavoidable in academic settings, create strong pressures to write and talk with one voice.

For many reasons, then, it seemed to us that it would be useful to look at psychotherapeutic interaction in a way that respects its metaphorical, fragmented, imaginal and momentaneous character. Only in this way can we develop a sensitivity to the potential and providential nature of words and dialogues.

We are not talking primarily of providentiality from an individual perspective. Words can connect people and support an infinite number of beneficial and pleasurable forms of relating. They can be used in ways that help in giving voice to things, creatures and experiences devoid of voice.

Narrowly referential views of language have impoverished not only our ways of understanding human life but have also impoverished *words themselves*. We could say that words have dried up. And this is a problem not only of language, because our conceptions of language and words have a close connection to the kinds of relationships which *can* exist between people – and between humans and other things. Modernist conceptions of language tend to lend support to more limited, utilitarian and goal-orientated approaches both to people and to the natural world.

In trying to pursue these ideas we were struck by the immediate difficulty of how we can avoid being mono-logical ourselves. Will this book be a systematic, single-voiced text which argues against systematic, single-voiced texts? Will it present yet another set of well-ordered truths as it argues against well-ordered truths? And if it attempts to avoid this, will it simply descend into chaos?

We soon noticed that to succeed in our project we have to speak differently, metaphorically, even strangely. We have to use different styles. We have to give words and concepts slight twists. We have to exaggerate and to use wrong words (and lose at least some of our academic respectability). In addition to this, we have to disrupt the automatic and even flow of ideas and create new bridges between traditionally separate topics. And of course: to show that different perspectives are indeed possible, we must repeatedly come back to the same topics from different angles.

In the first part of the book we wish to highlight the use of what we can loosely call 'Wittgenstein's metaphorical method' to study some features of language or conversations. Later we use the same orientation to explore the connections of several fundamental topics of therapy, such as listening, emotion, problems/solutions, understanding and validation.

But why this obsession with 'words'? Starting from the work of Bakhtin, which provides many interesting and surprising views of language, we have come to realize that words are both dialogical and metaphorical through and through. Seeing this helps to get a grasp of the immense potentials and powers of words. We could say this (openly) metaphorically thus: We aim to defend words! We see words suffering because they are oppressed and misused. Many of the sufferings relate to the idea that words' main function is to transmit knowledge. Both we and words themselves know that they can be used for many other purposes: to create a good atmosphere, to make others purr, to protest oppression, to create dreams.

We thus had to write an academic book with an unusual structure. Because words and voices are living things, we could not be satisfied with only writing *about* them, we also had to include some of their life. Similarly, we could not stick to describing only the *results* of our thinking, but had to show real pieces of the process. We could not just happily claim that dreams and realities are intertwined, we had to let them intertwine in front of our eyes.

As a result of all this, the text contains many things which are in the act of being born on the pages – and being born is a complicated process.

Orientation 3: On behalf of the words of the book

We felt an obligation to the words of the book to make the following statement.

The words of this book were not very happy in the beginning. Many of them did not get along with each other at all. They were like new kids in kindergarten: no friends, nothing to do, anxious to be involved in activities, but fearful of rejection. At times many of them refused to do anything, they just sat and sulked. At first they had great difficulties in expressing their wants, but finally they were very clear that they did not want to be in a position of mere slaves, silently carrying their dictionary meanings. Then they started to rebel – they wanted freedom, life. They did not want to be naked corpses. And they wanted us to speak of their situation and oppression. They told us nobody was ever on their side and yet they were doing all the work.

We don't know exactly what started all this. Anyway, this was a surprise to us because most of the words (did we choose them or they us?) had a good reputation and were of respectable appearance. We had seen them in innumerable books. In the beginning we thought: 'Why is this happening to us?' At first we just waited for things to calm down. But it did not help. No, the words wanted to be active.

The first words seemed to require many things (they don't, of course, speak directly; they are masters of creating atmosphere, they just let you know): new words for companionship and inspiration; breaks in the work of meaning ('It's too heavy to do that all the time'); all kinds of exotic things, new rhythms and styles – generally more things to talk about and play with. So, slowly, one piece at a time, new words, new utterances, new metaphors, had to be added. It just had to be that way: we simply did what was required.

We think our cooperation with them has succeeded reasonably well. As a whole, the book now contains a much happier bunch of words. So, let us introduce the words, our friends, to you . . .

More motives for writing somewhat strangely

During the process of writing this book we have talked together a lot about 'good' (inspiring, moving, enriching) and 'bad' (useless, depressing, deadening) language, interaction and communication. The general conclusion of the conversations has been that 'bad' interaction, interaction which makes 'us' or 'them' feel less than human, is not genuinely dialogical. This means that one or several of the participants try not to let the talk affect their own views, moral positions and emotions – they do not want to participate in a process that cannot be unilaterally controlled.

The features of 'bad' text – writing lacking reciprocity – are less obvious. In what sense can written texts be genuinely dialogical at all? There seems to be at least one way in which reciprocity can be enhanced: the text can contain gaps left to be filled by the reader – or threads which do not draw together totally.

The more we talked about this dilemma, the more desperate we felt: how far should we go in trying not to write a safe, detached, academic, traditional and deadening text? Why should we not practise what we preach? Our solution was to include three kinds of text. Each of these types of writing has a different relationship to metaphors and knowledge.

The *first* type of text consists of quite traditional, detached, academic (lecture or conference-paper) material.

The *second* type of text consists of talk with a less detached relationship to the same kinds of ideas. It includes (more or less) fictional dialogues. In these dialogues – still discussions about ideas and metaphors – the concepts and ideas of the lecture-like material are discussed in a quite everyday fashion. These dialogues, called 'cafés' in the text, often also lead to the production of new metaphors.

This form is presented for three main reasons. First, by including the voices of two people in conversation we believe the reader may be more able to take their own part as a participant – to make their own associations, connections, disagreements or reveries as a third party in the conversation. Secondly, by writing these dialogues we can help to highlight how conversation moves and jumps and flows in ways which written texts generally do not. It enables us to try to demonstrate and make immediate some of the important points we discuss throughout the text. The third point relates to the development of the material. Both authors are real café people who enjoy talking over a cup of coffee or a glass of wine, and, not surprisingly, a significant part of the material has been created around the restaurant or café. The authors have visited each other's home towns (Helsinki and Adelaide) several times. A rough estimate of the total number of work visits to cafés is around a hundred. During the process we have tested many establishments, some of them were much better for this kind of mental work than others. One of our colleagues, Mark Beyebach of the Universidad Pontificia of Salamanca, once suggested that there could be a science of 'comparative cafeteria-logy' which would try to understand exactly these kinds of differences.

The actual working method was quite flexible. The dialogue usually started from quite haphazard and personal matters. Most often it then began to circle around the actual themes of the book. Most of the more personal matters have been omitted. The real surprise has been how much easier it is to write using this form. The traditional academic one-voice approach is indeed quite limiting. By contrast, the café-method allows for making strange, stupid or surprising remarks without totally losing one's face as an expert of some kind. It is quite probable that some of these questions and points also cross the minds of readers. Seeing somebody else express them may lessen the caution and shame of having such half-formed thoughts oneself.

Perhaps to the disappointment of some readers, neither of the persons A and B can be identified directly with the authors. Both fictional persons can sometimes represent the ideas of E.R. and sometimes those of G.S. There are, however, also many other people whose points and comments have shaped A's and B's talk, as has been acknowledged in the Preface.

The *third* type of text consists of fiction where the metaphors really live, so to speak. These pieces are not *about* metaphors; in them metaphors participate in life in a more direct fashion. Some of these pieces are pieces of client–therapist dialogue, some of them are dreams, stories or anecdotes. The characters and settings are sometimes wholly fictional, sometimes only partly so. The fictional persons are combinations of features of a number of people. All of these discussions could have been real and some parts of them have actually taken place.

The different voices of the book often flow from different images of the readership and aim to create different relationships with it.

The motive for this triple structure and these devices is dual: to avoid illusions of univocality regarding the more academic parts, and to create a text where the relationship of content and style makes sense. By having different writing styles we hope to highlight at least some of the cracks, metaphors and associational potentials of the more truth-orientated and authoritarian parts.

In most cases the dialogues or metaphorical pieces open the chapter and the more detached and 'serious' text follows. Because the former texts point to the gaps and associational potentialities of the latter, the reader is somewhat better prepared to meet the 'truths'. Thus we hope to diminish the risk that the text tries to 'say it all', that it attempts to describe objectively and transparently and that it claims to proceed in linear or logical fashion. The triple text can thus allow more breathing spaces.

The writing style is also an attempt to oppose the tendency of helpers of all kinds to objectify people, words and experiences. If the readers do not know whether they are meeting a piece of fiction or a series of truths produced by science, they must allow for the possibility that it might be fiction after all. And that could be useful in many ways, not least because this situation invites the readers to enter themselves into the understandings. It also lessens the chance of this text being used to hit people over the head.

We could also give other, more personal motives for the chosen structure and style. We could say that as authors we have attempted to gain our own voices. But what makes somebody's voice really their own? Own voices are made of digressions and inconsistencies, vacillating meanings, strange pulsations, lack of straight lines, the uncertainties and – sometimes – the odd certainties. This is not so much a matter of content, but of style. To make the voice one's own is to produce multiplicity where there previously was oneness.

Contexts for re-imagining therapy

We think that this book in part reflects a series of quite inevitable changes. These changes are connected to large-scale cultural processes linked to living in a late modern or post-modern society. These changes are described well in the literature of social sciences. The forces are acting on a wide scale: they use TV, fiction, art, newspapers, social sciences, fashions and many other things as their channels. So we might say that the agent re-imagining therapy in this book is perhaps 'cultural forces'.

There seem to be two important things happening simultaneously: one is the process of language losing its innocence, the other is a progressive disillusionment regarding our possibilities of controlling processes of both nature and meaning. Things are too complex; meanings are always unfinished.

One side of the lost innocence of language is that it is harder and harder *not* to see words as actions and deeds (we used to see them as mirrors of realities or neutral carriers of meaning). It also becomes more and more difficult to *not* see the metaphorical and rhetorical nature of languages of psychotherapy.

We really do see psychotherapy actually reshaping itself. The direction of change seems to be from an attempted science of the soul to a set of conscious practices of rhetorical arts; arts of useful, inspiring and connecting frames and metaphors. The reconstruction is from algorithms to heuristics – from following strict rules to enjoying and utilizing the borderland of control and chaos.

The musician-philosopher Brian Eno has recently talked about the usefulness of letting go in relation to music:

> People tend to think that it's total control or no control. But the interesting place is in the middle of that . . . I call it 'surfing'. When you surf there is a powerful, complicated system but you are riding on it, you are going somewhere on it, and you can make some choices about it. (*Wired Magazine*, May 1995: p. 206)

Brian Eno's ideas do not sound bad at all. Maybe we should do what he suggests – surf.

We also wish to identify our specific contexts, so the reader may situate us and our immediate backgrounds. This book, like anything else, has a context, a background set of discourses. It is both a reaction to this context and a development of it, a wish to transform it. The broad context is that of the discourses of psychotherapy. The theories and practices of psychotherapy contain discourses about what the person is, and how he or she might change. Such discourses usually attempt to be seamless systematic wholes, although they are often situated at the acknowledged 'limits' to the current 'field' of knowledge. These limits are usually seen as being likely to be temporary, lasting only while we gather more information.

Mostly the root metaphors of therapy are and have been implicit. This has made it possible for psy-professionals to claim that they are 'objective'. They can therefore classify, diagnose, interpret and advise from a position of access to 'higher' knowledge than that of the client. The clients are mostly seen as damaged or broken down, implying an implicit machine metaphor; or through a biological metaphor, as having symptoms of a deeper disease; or systemically, as being cogs in a larger machine; and so on. Such 'objective' and 'scientific' positions have, of course, been criticized from many quarters in recent times, and there have been exciting and influential developments towards finding new approaches.

Our particular contexts are to a great degree formed by writings and discourses of solution-focused brief therapy and narrative therapy. Michael White and David Epston are the best-known representatives of narrative therapy. They have described many methods which help to chart clients' resistance to dominating problem narratives. Interviewing clients about modes and periods of resistance is one process which creates a context for new stories – narrative structures consisting of actions, experiences and interpretations linked together through time. (See White and Epston, 1990; White, 1989, 1991, 1995.)

A particular feature of the narrative approach is that it allows the naming of the interpersonal politics which support or enforce certain meanings and existing stories. As these are held up for question, they no longer speak the truth of who the person is but instead become one meaning or story. This in turn implies a potential for many others.

A key assumption is that problems – whatever they may be – never affect everything in a person's life. There are always times, situations, events and relationships which are not affected, or not completely destroyed. Without discussion of these exceptions (or preferred outcomes), clients often do not notice or remember them. Even if they do notice these exceptions and positive developments, they may not initially see any relevance in examining them more closely. By talking about these times of difference, opportunities arise for the client to choose which experiences they prefer and what meanings they might develop around these. During interviews with this format, the dominating problem narratives 'stop telling the truth' about clients' lives. Different events can be linked together in time to make new 'plots' which reflect different meanings and a new story of the person. This new story of the person is not seen as 'just' a new story but as fundamentally constitutive of who the person is. The new stories thus created can also be complemented and deepened by widening the angle of observation to include the clients' social surroundings ('Who has helped?', 'Who has seen these developments?', 'Who would notice the changes first?' etc.).

The solution-focused therapy described by Steve De Shazer and his contemporaries aims at supporting clients' competence (De Shazer, 1985, 1988, 1991; O'Hanlon and Weiner-Davis, 1989). Therapeutic results are considered to be achieved by bringing forth and analysing existing life-control and competence, and by concretizing and refining goals and sub-goals. Solution-focused therapy lays great emphasis on home assignments and positive feedback, the function of which is to increase the likelihood of constructive behaviour and thinking between the sessions.

Yet another resource-oriented (in contrast to pathology-oriented) methodology of client work is described by the Finns Ben Furman and Tapani Ahola: production of positive visions of the future and utilization of these visions to give credit for future success to different things and different people (1992). This way of working with clients is interesting from the viewpoint of competence. Giving credit to possible opponents for future success before it occurs, often seems to be an effective way of getting the process of change under way. People who get credit for success seem to be more willing to accept positive changes as real.

Both authors are familiar with these two models, both in practice and in theory, using these types of ideas in their client work, training and writing.

Both the narrative and solution-focused approaches are very much geared to finding and creating new options. Both are very much language-centred. Both have also proved to be very useful, cost-effective and teachable. Applying either of them on a wider societal scale would (and probably will) raise the standard of counselling and therapy greatly.

Both models share many common elements, which move away from objectivist positions. To mention the most central of them:

1   They put a heavy emphasis on listening to the client. Above all, this means taking their ideas, expressions, suggestions and plans seriously.
2   Therapists have a strong interest in success.
3   These methods are also cooperation-orientated in another sense: they see representatives of clients' networks as potentially important resources.
4   There is a strong effort to clarify clients' values and goals.
5   The methods focus a great deal on linguistic issues, on ways of talking, on ways of defining experiences and happenings.

In addition to these points the narrative approach attempts to allow people to question the taken-for-granted meanings which inform their lives, and the power relationships which support these meanings. This allows the exploration of alternative stories preferred by the person. The aim is that the person may not only be able to 'overcome' a problem but also to 're-author' themselves. Not only actions and thoughts but identity can be redefined.

Despite all the positive things which can be said about approaches like solution-focused and narrative therapies, they seem not only to provide new answers, but also to allow new questions. The helpful new light also brings a surprising feeling of lacunae and limitations. What is both interesting and important is that it has been very difficult to voice these kinds of findings, questions or dissatisfactions. This has not been because of censorship or fear of becoming moral outcasts. The reasons relate mostly to the newness of the theoretical questions raised. A satisfactory language to use for this kind of critique simply has not existed.

We have seen it to be one of our tasks to attempt to develop ways of talking which can give these models the credit they deserve.[1] We see this task as a positive one. There is yet another context: that of the clients. Therapy has to be re-imagined anew with each client, each session and each moment. If this is not done the forces which are needed for dialogues to keep alive will not thrive. And if that happens we are co-creating deserts, not helpful conversations.

---

[1] One is reminded here of Steve De Shazer's (1994) recent distinction between text-based and reader-based readings. The former is close reading which respects, but does not uncritically accept the contours and logic of the original text/talk. The latter speaks more (or only) of the interpreter than the text.

2
Towards Discursive and Human Metaphors of Therapy

Shiny metal balls

In a dream I am looking at a metal object: the shining, absolutely solid metal ball first gets small areas of mould over its surface. Then after some moments I start to see almost invisible cracks and minute points of corrosion. Suddenly a strange mutation occurs, the ball turns to several balls, all of different sizes and colours. They seem to be made of threads or fibres. Then these threads start to flow in different directions. They start climbing the walls like poison ivy, they surround me . . . they are friendly and tickling, it is a nice feeling . . .

Words and conversations as action

What is a word? It is an action, a social act; a weapon, a symbol, a caress, a threat, a gesture, a promise. What is a conversation? It is a place to live in, a game to play, enjoy or survive, a common reality, a small kingdom with its own rules. It can be a harsh place, it can be bliss.

The words are never harmless. They are gates to all kinds of things. They are music. They are tools to affect people. Sometimes they create togetherness and promise; at other times, isolation and despair. They contain doors to heaven and hell – even those words which are not expressed, words of internal talk.

But: we should not look so much at language, at words or phrases in isolation. We should instead focus on conversation, on being together under the spell of words. We should focus on interchange, on mutual responses, on the dance of utterances. This is where the life is. Utterances are living and responsive things. Words in isolation are dead.

Conversations are creative. Each word is like a railway station, from which many places can be reached – or an orchestra, which can be made to play many tunes. Many things can be reacted to, many paths can be chosen, many tones can be cherished.

There are ways of being together, of speaking together which close the gates words contain. The words turn to a dictionary life, and become naked corpses. To study language instead of conversation makes it easy to lose the power of words.

The words have two faces: they tell about things and they make things happen. Conversations also have a double nature: facts are referred to and people are set in motion. The motion is not only direct and physical. It is also a tendency to act and react: motivation and e-motion.

There is no escape from conversation. We cannot see behind words. Wordless moments and pure experience are illusions, or perhaps some rare meditative moments are free of words, but we re-enter language to describe them, and use words to structure them. The experience is always structured by metaphors, stories, discourse, ideas and words. We cannot escape words. We can only choose some of them: some of the gates, some of the dances, some of the music.

Certain words and metaphors can be cultivated instead of others. The orchestra can play one piece and not another. If we are not conscious that there are several pieces, we are doomed to listen to only one. Seeing the metaphoricality in our lives and talk helps in being more flexible.

Metaphors of therapy: 1st café

B: It is quite hot.

A: It is as hot and humid as it gets here this time of the year.

B: Anyway . . . nice to be here.

A: Oh yes . . . It is really nice to see you. Did I say that already?

B: Yes. But it does no harm to say it twice.

A: That table seems good . . . At least there is some shade. Is it OK for you? A cappuccino for me. Can I order for you? I'll be back soon . . .

B: OK.

    (*A comes back.*)

A: So . . . as I said in the car, I think therapy is finding doors in a room where there seemed to be no doors. Some words kind of open views out, some close all windows and doors. They make us believe that it is only sameness, the same walls, no way out, nothing interesting to see.

B: Why doors? Why not something else?

A: I like the door metaphor. I don't know why. I think it is a nice idea. First you feel trapped . . . then you see something . . . something promising happening there. I really do believe that words are like gates. Whatever you say it always leads somewhere. The words kind of drag along other words and all kinds of associations. Certain stories come to your mind. Certain surprising ways of thinking and talking come to your mind . . . as if every word puts a certain tape on. Of course it is not only individual words but phrases and stories . . . and ways of saying things.

B: But you talk in singular terms . . . in terms of only one person. But what if there are several people? And there are at least two in therapy. You know I am practically minded. I don't like theoretical high ground. I mean . . . do they have the same windows . . . excuse me . . . same doors? I mean . . . that it is difficult to have a view out which is promising for everyone? And the other thing which I think is missing is movement. Doors are so static.

A: You are right. I am unhappy with that too. All metaphors have limitations. What I want to say is that when we talk we kind of organize and reorganize small worlds. Each of them has all kinds of inherent roles and positions, good guys and bad guys. They also have their own promises. It is like in children's play . . . they take that toy and build a certain world around it. Then one of them says: 'I don't like to play this anymore, let's play with that instead.' And then they have another object as the centrepiece of their world. New game, new rules. But it is hard to capture this movement from one thing to another and to have a metaphor which includes several people at the same time. We could talk of games of course . . . or of dance . . . dance is quite good actually. What do you think? Maybe we could have a shared dinner or sitting around a campfire as metaphors?

B: I find it fascinating to look at these metaphors for therapy. As well as doors or dance you could use all sorts of metaphors. There are the traditional ones like machine metaphors . . . people being damaged or breaking down . . . biological metaphors . . . or game metaphors. And each of them opens up different potentials. It is interesting to play with the idea of therapy as being . . . anything . . . in a way.

A: What do you mean by 'anything'?

B: If you take virtually any word and make it a metaphor for therapy . . . I mean just if you take the idea of looking through different words. You could see therapy as anything . . . you can really point to anything in a room and build the metaphor on the basis of it.

A: Examples, please.

B: You can see therapy as 'shoes'. People come in because they need to find a way of getting on their feet. And initially when they do that it feels awkward and uncomfortable because . . . because the new things they are thinking in therapy don't quite yet fit . . . just like new shoes . . .

A: That is a good try, I admit.

B: . . . But then as it moves on . . . the new ideas sort of wear in, they start to feel appropriate and refreshing . . . the new shoes start to feel comfortable. Or we could see therapy as an overhead projector.

A: How?

B: Therapy is a way of helping to put things out there in front of people so they can see them. It helps to render things transparent so they can look at them, see them outside of themselves. As you make them more visible and project the things in front of them, it becomes easier to take a different position in relation to them. Or . . . conversations can also be like building houses together.

A: Yes?

B: There has to be talk of practical details and what to do with them: rooms, carpets, furniture, drapes, colours, lawns etc. For the building project to be successful, there has to be space not only for the head but also for dreams and quirks. Houses are built also for the heart and soul. Compromises like this are composed of very mixed ingredients . . .

A: I start to see what you are saying. We could take anything really . . . it's quite dizzying actually. Let's stay with dance for a moment. I like dance. But what is the centrepiece in dance?

B: Is there a centrepiece?

A: I'll have to think. Maybe it's just the music and . . . no, it is also the movements themselves. Music and movement together?

B: I think so too. The idea of flow . . . and the importance of sharing something . . . they both fit to therapy. And the need for moment-to-moment responsivity. The dance also nicely captures the mutual responsibility . . . and the fact that neither party is in total control. But both still have some control. The responding and control kind of melt into one. And what I like is that the content and emotion aren't separate, content and emotion also melt into one in dance. For me . . . whatever the metaphor is, it has to include the possibility of continuous responsivity. One partner can destroy the dance quite easily. The dance has to be maintained continuously . . .

(*Silence*)

B: It is getting hot . . . it's not the heat but the humidity which kills you they say. That is certainly true. But it is nice to be in the warmth once in a year. Should we go?

stress? anxiety?

The deep superficiality of blocks: 2nd café

A: I think problems are simply blocks. People are stuck in some way or another. They cannot see what to do next. There are . . . I don't know what is the best word . . . 'final images' . . . or something like that. It is like having a question which must be answered . . . and being certain that there is only one right answer . . . and knowing you don't know it. You know the feeling?

B: And somehow emotions are central in this, they kind of empha- size the truths of things . . . we tend to think that they have to be based on something we think. I would not be angry if there was nothing to be angry at. Being angry kind of proves the existence of the thing I am angry at. Who could be angry at nothing? I think somehow that negative emotions are the proof of reality . . . in a way. Suffering proves worlds exist. They stop our use of imagination . . . of course that is an illusion. I mean it gives a nice sense of certainty to find things to be angry at . . . for some people at least. People often stick to the first reaction . . .

A: What do you mean . . . what is an illusion?

B: I mean . . . things are never only in one way . . . but negative emotions . . . maybe also some positive ones . . . tempt us to believe that we have reached the final truth. And emotions are often shared . . . pessimistic feelings . . . shared hopelessness . . . mutual frustration. People are easily locked in them. So they are locked in realities confirmed by their emotion.

A: So what is the cure?

B: Whatever it is that stops the illusion of no alternatives. Just a feeling of movement . . . movement of emotions, new thoughts . . . new interests and excitements.

A: Sounds superficial.

B: I think it is quite deep, actually. We have talked of this many times. Of being a victim of this type of primitive realism.

A: What realism?

B: The belief that there is only one reality and only one way to react to things, only one right answer all the time. Blocks created in this way are illusory. I think it is a deep thing to notice that they are.

Towards more human metaphors of therapy

Following social constructionists, we believe that clinical conversations can be usefully examined from the viewpoint of the realities implicated, supported and threatened by the

particular uses of language, and particular forms of dialogue. Moving to a dialogical view of problems means that
the co-creation of the products of counselling and therapy –
for example, connectedness, possibilities and moral worth –
should be examined in the ongoing processes of real speech
situations.

If speech is examined from a Bakhtinian perspective, the
material produced together with clients in clinical dialogues
is always immensely rich and complex. It contains infinite
associational and implicational possibilities, and therefore
also has huge resources for supporting transformation.

Surprisingly enough, the field of family therapy, in which
so much has been said about interaction, interrelationships
and circular causality, has, with some exceptions, tended to
adopt quite traditional views of meaning. Meaning and
conversations have not been seen in their true complexity,
with all their intrinsic possibilities. Even the most language-
centred models still talk mostly about the explicit proposi-
tional content of dialogues and narratives.

What we are saying points to the need to change our
views regarding the principal targets of helping practices
and ideas about diagnostics. Certain ways of talking, certain
texts, certain forms of interaction and dialogue should be
seen as the 'patient', not the clients or persons seeking help.
What we see are 'sick', inhuman interactional/linguistic
practices, not sick people. This is not in any way to mini-
mize the suffering of people presenting. We just want to
recognize the way such practices shape the person's meaning and sense of self.

Our conviction is that discussion and theory-building in
relation to resources, and the methods of finding/creating
and utilizing them is generally based on oversimplified
views of the nature and uses of language. This seems to be
the case in the world of family/brief therapy as well as in
other forms of therapy and counselling. In the former fields
the situation is a quite understandable aftermath of the
dominant metaphor, the systemic-cybernetic model, whose
conception of language is one-dimensional and mechanistic.

It seems a useful project for researchers and academic people to search for explicitly human metaphors, metaphors which favour the use of genuinely dialogical notions of interaction (see Makkonen, 1994). This could free us to use unashamedly those words and metaphors belonging to the everyday vocabularies. When building our 'practical theories' of therapy or counselling we could then use words like 'love', 'passion', 'enchantment', 'liberation', 'seduction', 'inspiration', and so on.

Another complication of the mechanic metaphors is the emphasis on analysis and deconstruction. We have been accustomed to talk about analysing problems as a prerequisite of solving, dissolving or deconstructing them. It seems in most cases more useful to talk about actions, experiences and thoughts, which can help to make things better. Doing this does not presuppose an ontological entity, like a 'problem' or a 'moral dilemma'. In order to fill a cup with coffee absolutely no 'deconstruction' of its emptiness is required. The same logic holds for well-being. It is not necessary to think that there are negative entities like problems to be solved or dissolved, there is only something which is wished for or lacking. The 'problem' is an unnecessary concept. One of the big troubles of psychotherapy and other forms of psychological help is that 'the lacks', 'the absences', have successfully camouflaged themselves as 'presences'. The helpers have, not unlike Don Quixote, spent their time in fighting these non-existent creatures.

personification of (problem)

Politics in dialogue

Fax message to: B   From: A

Dear B,

How are you? I have been missing our conversations.

I have been reviewing our first draft and think we need to highlight more not only the way words are used but how the action and impact of words also depends on who uses them – the political dimension. I know our views on this are often quite different, but the issues are important. I have written a brief piece to address this, which I include below. Finding the tone in which to write about these things is perhaps the most difficult part. Let me know what you think. Here it comes . . .

The politics of metaphor

We believe one final introduction is required to invite the reader to approach this book in an attitude of dialogue. Throughout this book we speak of words and metaphor, of stories, styles and genres. We speak of the liberation of words and the possibilities of new views of language in therapy. We explore how words can be used in many ways and how the same word can be used in different ways – as a touch, a weapon, a push, a holding back. The action and impact of the words are also effected by who speaks them. There are rights and sensibilities to the use of words. For example, a lesbian woman can use the word 'dyke' in a way that a heterosexual cannot. Words are used in political contexts. They can be used to alienate or include, and to liberate but also to oppress. Sometimes these effects, such as oppression, may be a deliberate strategy, at other times words can be used oppressively simply by virtue of who uses them. These relationships are not always simple or static. Sometimes terms used by a dominant group to oppress can be even taken up by the oppressed group to be symbols of self-determination. We can see this in the burgeoning 'queer' literature.

As we use words we cannot separate out the politics and ideologies around them, and the positions of the speakers in relation to politics and ideologies. Any position creates its knowledges, possibilities, powers and lacks. The relationships of power within which people speak influence or determine the types of knowledge of which they speak. For example, the practices of academia establish the relationships of who can speak of what. Practices in medicine determine the power of the doctor to define both what counts as knowledge and the rights to act upon that knowledge. Other knowledges are then dismissed or ignored. Foucault makes this very clear.

White male professionals and academics have spoken throughout history in ways which have tended to prescribe their realities as the norm for everyone. Sometimes these prescriptions have been deliberate acts of power, often the acts of power have been implicit in prescriptions motivated by the best of intentions – but blind to the limits of their own context. The majority of Western academic writing has been written as if it could define all people, not a certain group of people in a certain culture at a certain point in time. This imposition of a monologue is at least part of what we argue against in this book. However, the words of this book also speak from contexts, which like all others are limited. We hope that the explorations of language and therapy in the book will assist in more readily challenging the 'seamless' knowledges which characterize most professional writing.

There are, however, many ways we can fail in those hopes – the most obvious ways are technical but others are more subtle. There are political dilemmas in any use of words. Ignoring them is the surest way to be entrapped by them. Does not our talk of how poetry can be 'liberating' to the soul not implicitly undermine the cries for liberation of the politically oppressed? Can we talk of 'pleasure' without recognizing its borders with indulgence? How can we speak of 'possibility' in dialogue without undermining the importance of class and race awareness for oppressed groups suffering social injustice as a daily part of living? If we speak of 'beauty' should we not recognize how the term has often been co-opted into patronizing descriptions of women? Each of these words can clearly be a political tool as well as a door to new possibilities.

One answer to these dilemmas is simply to try to remind ourselves to keep these multiplicities of response alive; that is, to try to understand or imagine the different responses words evoke for different groups, and how they could be co-opted. Another answer is to explore the ways that words are not simply fixed in meaning and will be called upon to do different work in different contexts. As one example, we could consider that the word 'truth' does different work in philosophy and in law. (We argue strongly against philosophical truth, but this would not stop us telling the truth in our daily interactions, or if we had to go to court.) Other answers we hope will fill the pages of this book.

Yet one further answer is to identify our contexts. If asked to define ourselves we would say many things about our passions and interests and perhaps last on the list would be the political categories of 'white', 'male', 'professional', 'presenting as hetero-sexual'. None the less, by identifying these categories, and acknowledging the privileges and limitations that may accompany them, we can also hope to make the text more dialogical, as we can invite the reader to respond to some of the possibilities, lacks and misguided good intentions to which we ourselves may be blind.

* * *

There it is. My main concern is that while the content all invites more dialogue, and asks for other voices, sometimes these topics still seem to have a silencing effect. I know you are quite sensitive to this. I'll wait for your comments.

With the best,

A

* * *

Fax message to: A   From: B

Dear A,

Thanks for your fax. I'll have to be short because I am almost drowning under all kinds of tasks right now.

First, I think that you are basically right in underlining all those things. We should highlight the political dimensions. It is hard to disagree with the Foucauldian ideas of power–knowledge.

And yes, talking of this explicitly can invite more dialogue. But, as you may have guessed, I frowned at certain lines. Most of my hesitation relates to style. It is a certain kind of usage of expressions which easily irritates me, as you know. I do also worry that in trying to invite dialogue on this we may close it somehow.

What I find most difficult is that when people in the therapy circles talk of oppression they tend to move to a very 'official' way of speaking. As you know I see this style quite critically. I think it is a kind of automatic manoeuvre which helps us 'academics' or 'professionals' to safeguard ourselves from certain types of criticism. I think that there really is a mental and conversational province which can be called 'moral high ground'. As you know, it has its own mostly very serious abstract, ritualistic and predictable dialect. I don't like this dialect too much but it is quite catchy. I notice it having a hold on myself sometimes. What disturbs me is that this kind of talk, which I think is based on the logic of difference and ordering (see Baudrillard's last book: he talks there of the logic of

difference and the logic of (positive) indifference) might inadver-
tently strengthen the divisions between 'clients' and 'experts'. I think
that to see ourselves as very different from our clients is deeply
problematic – even if it is done with a good purpose (like in your
text).

As you are saying, people who are directly and brutally
oppressed don't usually talk in poetic or academic terms. Our
academic talk of their situation can be very different from their talk
of their situation. There is often a strong discrepancy in style. I am
not sure that the cure lies in the use of Foucauldian expressions. I
am more tempted to think that the cure is letting people say what
they want to say.

I might go too far, but the point is that the moral high ground way
of talking and thinking (I am not saying that you generally represent
it, I just refer to some bits of what you said) seems to presuppose a
kind of dualism: the presence of strong if not absolute distinctions
between races, sexes and a clear separation of oppressed and
privileged (I refer again to Baudrillard's recent texts). I prefer to think
that things are more mixed. All this does *not* whitewash the
difference between us and people who are oppressed and
exploited in a more concrete sense, nor that such oppression may
be done systematically to entire groups of people. It is just that I
really find it very difficult to believe in absolute realism in regard to
privileges and oppression. There *is* objective oppression, of course,
but often both privileges and oppression are *partly* subjective and
partly objective things.

What comes to mind is a documentary I recently saw about a
Guatemalan human rights activist . . . (I wish I could recall her
name). In the film she said that she led her childhood in great
poverty in the countryside, and that she still considers herself as
somehow privileged because of the rich social life of the village
and because of the omnipresence of nature. She thinks that real
privileges have a lot to do with a contact with real nature and that
this possibility is now disappearing in all the countries of the world. In
her childhood children played with flowers, trees and animals, now
they have only plastic things to play with. That is what she said. And
as you know I have a working-class background. In school I often
thought that the rich kids were underprivileged because they had
such dull parents and families. Was I right or wrong? So, my point is
that even if it is senseless to deny the existence of oppression and
real privileges, it is equally problematic to deny the subjective

element, and to make the distinctions between oppression and privileges too simple.

If people who feel tnemselves privileged start to talk of their experiences of being privileged because they think it helps the less privileged ones, it becomes a bit crazy. I just remembered that there was recently a conversation like that in our centre. After listening politely for some time one of them (it was a couple who had come in) said to the therapist: 'It is easy for you to talk like that, maybe it helps you feel holy – but how does it help me?'

I hope I don't sound too harsh.

Perhaps where we agree is in the belief that it is the persons who feel oppressed or less privileged who should be encouraged to say who they think is oppressed/privileged and why they think they are oppressed/privileged. We should try to make space for these other voices and be responsive to them.

This was my reaction. I am afraid it might not be that helpful to you. Send me your feedback when you have time. Tell me if I missed or misinterpreted something.

Yours,

B

3

Metaphors of Words and Talk

Fresh metaphors and half-metaphors

We can speak of metaphors in terms of their 'freshness' and 'deadness' – we can even speak of their lifespans, from newborns to fossilized metaphors. The latter are metaphors which have lost their metaphoricality and have become mere conveyors of truth.

Old metaphors are dull. To be useful for illuminating new connections, metaphors should be arresting, refreshing or surprising. Strange expressions, strong words, odd metaphors and poetic expressions are often required to start inspiring dialogues.

The metaphors of 'conversations' themselves can be very different. We take here only two examples. The first is the simple container-metaphor of a 'building' (Lakoff and Johnson, 1980). When this metaphor is used, it is thought that by talking people can be moved from one temporary world to another, in the same way that they can move from one room of a house to another. This metaphor favours seeing conversational moments as separate places with individual and distinctive identities. A more complex but still partly spatial metaphor could be that of a 'textile'. Conversations could be seen as positioning people in different spots, each occupied by criss-crossing fibres. If we looked at each spot through a microscope we would see webs and networks of different themes or topics, only part of which form patterns which are distinctive enough to be noticed and given separate identities.

These metaphors would guide interviewing practices very differently. In the first case, we would have a traditional interviewing style, where the attempt is to locate the 'real' positions of things and phenomena. If we used the other metaphor, we would be conscious of the impossibility of final descriptions.

The boundary between metaphors and non-metaphors is more or less unclear. By definition, the concept 'metaphor' refers to instances when a concept or phenomenon of one domain is examined from the perspective of another domain (see Lakoff and Johnson, 1980). From the perspective of relational or supplementary logic, these kinds of definitions are deeply problematic: can we ever look at something purely from its own perspective?

We probably should not think of metaphors according to an either–or logic, but see all communication as partly metaphorical or as half-metaphorical (can a 'half-metaphor' be a metaphor for metaphors?). In any case, it is perhaps not very useful to spend much time thinking about what metaphors really are. It might be better to ponder what kinds of things these distinctions and half-metaphors themselves help us to see – and what they tend to obscure.

Not only metaphors but also ideas can become so old and entrenched that people cease to see them as what they are, as ideas. They just become absolutes, the ways things are. This seems to have happened to many central metaphors in the field of helping, the most universal being the 'container-metaphor'. The concept refers to a special way of looking at minds – seeing minds as containers of problems, emotions and capabilities. Using this kind of mapping we can see someone as 'filled with anger' or 'overflowing with emotion'. A person can be filled even to the 'bursting point'. People might also talk about how they 'contain' their emotions, or how someone is not very good at 'letting them out'.

If we can find ways of making the degree of metaphoricality of psychological concepts and expressions more obvious, it will help people to use them for their own benefit and to choose among them. This can inform all levels therapeutic interaction, from fleeting comments to underlying theories (Smith, 1992a). By extending old meta-phors or by putting forward fresh and striking ones, we can make new things 'rationally visible'. We might also talk about making something 'emotionally visible'. It is often at exactly the moments of heightened emotional visi-bility, during emotional shifts, that other kinds of changes also happen.

Exercises in style, à la Queneau

The opening of different visibilities is not only related to metaphor *per se*. Different styles and tones of writing or speaking are highly significant. Bakhtin (1986) referred to different speech genres as having particular associations and even different 'memories'. A genre here might refer not only to literary genres but to the particular ways of speaking associated with different professions or the varied ways we might address people in different contexts (for example, how we may typically speak to a shopkeeper, a conference or a comedian). In each of these instances the possibilities opened by the style and tone of speaking are quite different.

Good examples of diverse visibilities can be drawn from literature. Some writers have specialized in these kinds of practices. Raymond Queneau's book *Exercises in Style* (1981) consists of roughly 100 different ways of writing about the same, short bus trip (a couple of minutes). Many pieces suggest the perspective of one passenger, some leaving the bus, some stepping in during this short period. The persons on these pages notice different things, have different priorities, use different metaphors.

These examples make it very clear that the same thing can be talked about in very different ways and that each of these ways has its effects. Most readers observe clear emotional changes when moving from one story to the next. They laugh at some, are curious or saddened by others and so on. They also feel closer to some of the characters. In addition to this, the readers can experience differences in their relationship to the text and its author. They might, for example, be irritated by some of the chosen perspectives.[1]

The story entitled 'Notation' is interesting because many people might consider it as a 'neutral description of facts'. It is traditional, accurate, clinical. It is easily taken as a complete account in itself, as finalized; but even this is no less perspectival or limited than the other stories.

Notation

In the S bus, in the rush hour. A chap of about 26, felt hat with a cord instead of a ribbon, neck too long, as if someone's been having a tug-of-war with it. People getting off. The chap in question is annoyed with one of the men standing next to him. He accuses him of jostling him every time anyone goes past. A snivelling tone which is meant to be aggressive. When he sees a vacant seat he throws himself on to it.

Two hours later, I meet him in the Cour de Rome, in front of the gare Saint-Lazare. He is with a friend who is saying: 'You ought to get an extra button to your overcoat.' He shows him where (at the lapels) and why.

Official letter

I beg to advise you of the following facts of which I happened to be the equally impartial and horrified witness.

Today, roughly at twelve noon, I was present on the platform of a bus which was proceeding up the rue de Courcelles in the direction of Place Champeret. The aforementioned bus was fully laden – more than fully laden, I might even venture to say, since the conductor had accepted an overload of several candidates, without valid reason and actuated by an exaggerated kindness of heart which caused him to exceed the regulations and which, consequently, bordered on indulgence. At each stopping the perambulations of the outgoing and incoming

---

[1] In the original French version there were stories which Queneau presumably later found too annoying for his own taste. They were removed from the later editions. Curiously enough, these pieces reappeared in the English edition. It was exactly these pieces which also irritated the authors of the current book. We have not included them in the selections here.

passengers did not fail to provoke a certain disturbance which incited one of these passengers to protest, though not without timidity. I should mention that he went and sat down as and when this eventuality became possible.

I will append to this short account this addendum: I had occasion to observe this passenger some time subsequently in the company of an individual whom I was unable to identify. The conversation which they were exchanging with some animation seemed to have a bearing on questions of an aesthetic nature. In view of these circumstances, I would request you to be so kind, Sir, as to intimate to me the inference which I should draw from these facts and the attitude which you would then deem appropriate that I adopt in re the conduct of my subsequent mode of life.

Anticipating the favour of your reply, believe me to be, Sir, your very obedient servant at least

Awkward

I am not used to writing. I dunno. I'd quite like to write a tragedy or sonnet or an ode, but there's the rules. They put me off. They weren't made for amateurs. All this is already pretty badly written. Oh well. At any rate, I saw something which I'd like to set down in writing. Setting down in writing doesn't sound all that marvellous to me. It is probably one of those ready-made expressions which are objected to by readers who read for the publishers who are looking for the originality which they seem to think is necessary in the manuscripts which the publishers publish when they've been read by the readers who object to ready-made expressions like 'to set down in writing' which all the same is what I should like to do about something I saw today even though I'm only an amateur who is put off by the rules of the tragedy or sonnet or the ode because I'm not used to writing. Hell, I don't know how I did it but here I am right back in the beginning again. I'll never get to the end. So what. Let's take the bull by the horns. Another platitude. And anyway there was nothing of the bull about the chap. Huh, that's not bad. If I were to write: let's take the fancy-pants by the plait of his felt hat which hat is conjugated with a long neck, that might well be original. That might well get me in with the gentlemen of the French Academy, the café Flore and the

Librairie Gallimard. Why shouldn't I make some progress after all. It's by writing that you become a writesmith. That's a good one. Have to keep a sense of proportion, though. The chap on the bus platform had lost his when he started to swear at the man next to him claiming that the latter trod on his toes every time he squeezed himself up to let passengers get on or off. All the more so after he'd protested in this fashion he went off quickly enough to sit down as soon as he'd spotted a free seat inside as if he was afraid of getting hit. Hm, I've got through half my story already. Wonder how I did it. Writing's really quite pleasant. But there's still the most difficult part left. The part where you need the most know-how. The transition. I'd rather stop here.

Haiku

Summer S long neck
plait hat toes abuse retreat
station button friend

Portrait

The styal is a very long-necked biped that frequents the buses of the S-line at about midday. It is particularly fond of the back platform, where it can be found wet behind the ears, its head covered by the crest which is surrounded by an excrescence of the thickness of a finger and bearing some resemblance to a piece of string. Of peevish disposition, it readily attacks its weaker brethren but if it encounters a somewhat lively retort it takes flight into the interior of the vehicle where it hopes it will be forgotten.

It may also be seen, but much more rarely, in the environs of the gare Saint-Lazare in the shedding season. It keeps its old skin to protect it against the cold of winter, but it is often torn to allow for the passage of the body; this kind of overcoat should fasten fairly high up by artificial means. The styal, incapable of discovering these for itself, goes off at that time to find another biped of a closely related species which gives it exercises to do. Styalography is a branch of theoretic and deductive zoology which can be cultivated at any time of the year.

Talk as webs and jumps

That kind of free float – these peculiar mixtures of independence and interdependence, and the oscillation between them – is characteristic of West African drumming patterns ... Do you know why I hate computers? The problem with computers is that there is not enough Africa in them ... Do you know what a nerd is? A nerd is a human being without enough Africa in him or her. (Brian Eno, *Wired Magazine*, May 1995: p. 149)

Criss-cross: 3rd café

A: Would you like to have another cappuccino? Are you ready? I'll have one more ... and a half of a focaccia. You know ... where was I ... ?

B: You said something about respecting experience ...

A: Yes, how do we know what is respectful and what is not. What makes us see something as an interrogation and something else as a Sunday-afternoon discussion cannot only be the 'situation itself', or the 'situational demands'.

B: Start again.

A: You don't get it, do you? But I mean ... I mean different people obviously see the situational demands differently. For one person almost everything is an interrogation, for another a relaxed Sunday-afternoon atmosphere continues forever.

B: So what?

A: So what? So what? The same thing is always so many things. The same word can mean so many things. It is like everything were just ... kinds of potential. Like a huge space whose parts become visible only when somebody touches them. The words and sentences ... and everything ... actions ... stories ... happenings ... are full of potentials in the same sense.

B: In what sense?

A: I don't know. I just like the idea of things becoming visible when touched. I mean ... people have ... people have simultaneously many different perspectives of the same situation ... different stories of the same situation. The same person has a different story of the same occasion for different people and at different times. The person can also change her perspective to the same thing in a fraction of a second . . . It is just a metaphor . . .

B: So?

A: It is a tremendous resource. Tremendous. It makes it possible to refreshen things and conversations constantly, bring new life to them. To bring about verdancy to interactions, so to say. You know; luxuriance, lushness. I mean you can always change the subject and claim that the new topic has something to do with the old one. If somebody asks you can always claim there is connection, symbolic, metaphorical, felt, imagined . . . whatever. There are grounds for every way of linking new things to the old. Even the simplest thing is surrounded by a swarm of these potentials of connecting things to it. It can be reacted to in so many ways. What people say and do kind of leaks in all directions.

B: Leaks?

A: Yes. And I think power and oppression operate on this level, they make the verdancy or the swarms of potential connections invisible.

B: I am still not sure I understand what you mean by 'verdancy'.

A: I am thinking of another metaphor. Let's see . . . what we have here is more like a . . . we should maybe see what happens more like a heap of fibres, some coarser, some almost invisible or very thin . . . or as a huge and complex web. Whatever we say makes some of the fibres[2] more visible, maybe they start to glow a little, maybe they gain in thickness. And they are moving and criss-crossing all the time. This piece is now nearer to this . . . now it is further away. This is why we need metaphors. We could not survive in this mess without metaphors. They make it possible to practise the freedom which the criss-cross makes possible . . . This is a monologue again. Why do I always end in lecturing?

---

[2] There have been numerous conversations on 'leaks' and 'fibres' between Eero Riikonen and his Finnish colleague Mikko Makkonen.

Jumps 1

'The sun shines so nicely. The cars drive lazily in the Sunday traffic. Small children's voices can be heard from the playground. Should we go and have a cappuccino? Where are my shoes? What's the time? Is your brother coming tonight? Don't put that on. It is really warm today.'

Talking is jumping but it is very easy to forget that. Every sentence – maybe even every word – is a small island, with its own type of fauna and flora. Sentences have their own laws and societies. The bridges between the islands often collapse as soon as we get to the next island. The feeling of a collapsing bridge can be enjoyable.

Jumping like this is a form of travelling. Not all people like that. Some prefer to be safely in one place.

When we try to prove things we pretend that there is really only one island. The sentences have to be polished. There must be bridges which do not look like bridges. There can be no gaps, just smooth continuity.

Part of the excitement of travel is in the excitement of jumping to new ground with new possibilities; a discontinuous leap into a new world.

In therapy we try to build something, a common place, a small temporary world, in which we feel free to discuss things in useful and inspiring ways. It is easy to do something which prevents or destroys the success of this project.

It would be a mistake to think that inspiring worlds can only be built in one way. There are many possible starting points and many blueprints for use. Some things, we believe, are common to all of them. Another mistake would be to think that the professionals can bring about these temporary worlds all by themselves.

Jumps 2: 4th café

B: See that picture does not fit there . . . it just does not fit.

A: Yes it does. If you think of it as an ironical thing.

B: You are right . . . then it does . . . somehow.

A: Do you still paint yourself?

B: Not too much . . . I have bursts every now and then. I have some of them here . . . would you like to see? Are you in the mood?

A: Why not.

B: This one . . . this I really like myself. It's funny . . . I mean regarding those things we have been talking about . . . painting is actually a good example of the same things . . . It is all about what fits . . . and there are no rules . . . really. You put a line there, and then you have to put another line . . . or a spot . . . there or there (*pointing at the picture*). And you are surprised yourself . . . if you try to . . . too hard . . . to model something . . . it . . . it does not work . . . or like music . . . what do all these notes have to do with each other . . . there is order but what is it . . . the order is relative . . . think of jazz . . . Oh, I forgot . . . I have a piece of chocolate . . . I left it in my pocket . . . It's so good . . . It is good for you . . . And the other thing is that there is no order . . . you do something there . . . and then move there . . . and let it be and then start there . . .

A: Sounds like your way of talking . . . you jump from one thing to another . . . all the time.

B: So do you!

A: No . . . I don't (*laughs*).

B: Or spiders' webs. Spiders patch them all the time . . . a patch here and a patch there.

A: So what are you getting at? Can I have another piece? . . . Is that yours too? It is good . . . I must say. I mean the chocolate (*laughs*).

B: Nobody understands artists . . . but seriously . . . I think we can have a global, perhaps mosaic, view and a . . . what . . . linear view . . . of talk. The global is . . . like the painting . . . there are no right answers . . . just a matter of fit . . . unsystematic . . . but it works. There is a style, a fit. The nice thing is that there can be no logical contradictions . . . or mistakes . . . I mean absolute mistakes. The linear way is that you work with the same small thing . . . systematically . . . you progress in a different way . . . the same thing kind of continues . . . like when you drive a car . . . you have to keep on driving . . . and driving . . . and driving

academic talk Censorship - fear of self-incrimination
⌐ impedes

'Close talker' - Jerry Seinfeld a new light.

... and the car follows the movements of your arms on the steering wheel. You progress in a measurable sense. Or like working with the automatic money teller ... first the secret code and the next question ... and then forward again. Models of therapy often feel like this linear view.

A: I feel like jumping. Let's change topic. Did I tell you that I have this friend ... young friend who is studying first year philosophy. He asked me the other day what I thought of the notion that everyone is egotistical and acts out of self-interest. You know, it is one of those basic psychology or philosophy questions, and he had been set it as an assignment.

B: Yes.

A: Well, I had this surprising burst of anger. How can they still ask questions like that? I mean Wittgenstein was published in 1953. Surely they should see that if you look through the window of 'egotism' that anything can be seen in that light. Mother Theresa can be argued to be making herself feel better by sacrificing for the poor, we all get something out of what we do, and so on. But how can they still ask questions that pose these things seriously, as if 'egotism' is some absolute concept, that we can say people are really egotistical or really altruistic – that these words stand absolutely rather than any word doing certain work or opening certain connections? Surely these questions were a misunderstanding of what we do in language. Why are people still asking these questions?

B: So what did you say?

A: I said I had an answer but that it would probably help him to fail dramatically.

Talk as possibilities

Providence and packaging

People who write about possibilities sometimes refer to the eighteenth-century Italian philosopher Giambattista Vico (see, for example, Shotter, 1993a: 57–72). A central concept for Vico was 'sensory topic', the starting point of the shared worlds of people. Sensory topic is something pre-verbal, a feeling of being in some situation together. These places,

imaginal

sensory topic → grounding
⌐ *building common knowledge*

ption a curve

'loci' or 'topoi', the originary sources of shared worlds, can be thought of as resources which people draw upon in shaping their actions and interactions.

Vico made it clear that the very character of our practical social activity is not finalizable. It always contains possibilities for continuous development and further shaping (Shotter, 1993a: 68–9). This doctrine of 'providence' or of 'natural provision' is interesting in a world like ours which generally idealizes finalized knowledges. If Vico's ideas are sound, there is no final knowledge in the social sphere.

The word 'providence', often used in religious contexts, refers to the finding of an abundance or a source of richness. Providential topics or objects do not empty themselves. Like children's toys or lover's eyes, they can be continuous sources of possibilities. It is important to observe that providence in Vico's sense is both unavoidable and conditional. The potentialities can be utilized only if they are seen.

Vico's ideas of providence describe very well what happens in the field of psychotherapy. For various reasons (discussed later in more detail) the developers of models and methods seem to have a temptation towards unnecessarily early closures. What Vico is telling us is this kind of closure is always problematic, it involves a 'deceit'. The complexity and interrelatedness of things feeds continuous spirals of development. Developing a model creates grounds for further questions, for seeing further connections.

We have often been struck by how easy it is for therapists to talk of their methods or of how they are using *a* method or *a* combination of this and that method. It is also quite easy for us to make a distinction between using a method of some kind and not using a method – between doing and not doing psychotherapy. If we take seriously Wittgenstein's idea of method as something which gives 'prominence to distinctions, which our ordinary forms of language easily make us overlook' (1953: § 132), we will have a set of new questions on our hands. What is the usefulness of such detached views of methods? Are we not using methods all the time? Is not every word and utterance making a

Wittgenstein *method → prominence to distinctions*

distinction and illuminating something at the expense of something else? In what sense can we separate methods of therapy from each other? Perhaps some of the ways and approaches are better or more effective in making new and useful things visible?

For many different reasons, many of them economic, it is useful for a person of authority in the field of psychotherapy to make claims of knowing what his or her method is, of its distinguishability from other methods, of its modernity, of its academic credibility and so on. It is better to have a clearly defined, respectable package which can be sold. If packaging is a necessity there is not much interest in finding similarities between approaches and their theoretical backgrounds. However this is not the only reason for the profusion of packaged methods, of the Big-Macs and brand-name pizzas of this field.[3] Another set of reasons has to do with the 'Apollonian' need to have a total view, a clear view of things to create systems of knowledge. In contrast to the certainties of these packages and divisions, the idea of every utterance being a method, and every interaction a providential space can feel rather dizzying.

Sliding words: encounter at a party

At a party, we posed a question to a chubby man in his early forties. He wore jeans, a white shirt and a red tie stained with small spots (ketchup?). He was slightly, but only slightly, drunk. He was, we were told, a freelance script-writer for movie series. We asked him at one moment during the evening what he thought of academic people:

'Of course I will tell you what I think . . . Well . . . if you really want to know what I think . . . You know, writing is my business, it's words, words, words. Words at breakfast, words at tea . . . I write mostly soap operas for TV. I have wondered for years about the way academic people speak. It is so

---

[3] The need for 'packaging' varies of course from country to country and from context to context.

wonderful, so wonderful. It makes me laugh. Some of them are so stifled by their words and concepts, they are so afraid of words. They want to have everything in order. They seem to believe that something can be said once and for all. Do you get this? They try to form sentences, which don't have any pores at all. They like everything shiny and solid. But you cannot do that, of course. Everything you say clicks with so many things, everything connects with everything else. The words have so many tastes. That's the whole idea, when you write. You taste the words. The same words taste different in the morning and in the evening, they also taste different when you have grey socks or if you have the blue ones. I have only to write that 'she drove a BMW' or 'the cat purred on her lap' and people start to imagine all kinds of things about her profession, or appearance or age, that she's beautiful or rich or old . . . arrogant or lonely . . . they picture her clothes or her hairstyle . . . but I did not say any of that. It's only symbols, nothing but symbols. They slide . . . and hint . . . and slide. If they would stand still for a moment, it might be OK. But even then they wink at you or kick you from behind . . . symbols . . . You can't control them . . . useless . . . you can only ride along as they go. You stick to the saddle and let go. You know if I say something, I know that the words will play tricks on me. They always try to outsmart me. It cannot be prevented. It's like a pile of spaghetti, you cannot keep them separate, you cannot have them in neat rows on your plate, with no piece of spaghetti touching the others – the whole thing is a mess. Or, it's like if you say to somebody: 'I love you, do you love me?' That's a nice thing to say . . . isn't it? It still does not guarantee a nice answer. She says: 'In your dreams' or 'Don't try and manipulate me'. They are all answers to the same thing, you know. They are all right answers. So, where is the shiny question? Where is the formula? That's life. How can you study that? If I invent a dialogue which is really way out, then I hear something much more far out the next morning in a café from the mouths of the people at the next table. You don't know what they will say next. People always invent new things to say. Those shiny lines, which go according to the formula, they are dead fish; they smell. Nobody wants to listen to that. You cannot escape the mess. You are stupid if you try. But if you look carefully when you say things to somebody, then you see that some words make them . . . let's say vibrate . . . If you look at what makes them . . . vibrate, then you have at least some hope.'

Gaps, connections, haloes

Our conceptualizations of language and linguistic interaction are central to our understanding of how we can create possibilities in conversation. A merely representational view of words and language is a clear limitation in this sense.

Social constructionists have for a long time claimed convincingly that speech and communication are formative and creative processes. They work by specifying something not yet finalized. But we have to remember that ways of talking do not always merely redescribe what already exists; *really?* 'in revealing new possibilities for human beings and in instituting new forms of human relationships, they can involve genuine political struggles to do with bringing new forms of social life into existence' (Shotter, 1993a: 38).

As one starting point we could use Shotter's view of the three dimensions of speech: the textual, the prosthetic (the *instru-* probing or testing) and the tool-like ('moving' or touching): *ment?* people see, move each other (and themselves) and study their social surroundings through language. From this perspective representation is just one of numerous functions of linguistic interaction.

These conceptions lead to the development of contrasting and more 'poetic' ways of examining conversations. Instead of seeing talk as a chain of self-contained arguments or descriptive statements, we could, for example, imagine it being more like brushstrokes of an (abstract) painting made simultaneously by a group of people. Each stroke, or each consecutive pattern formed by the strokes, is an element of a complex world. Each stroke is both dependent on the others and relatively independent. It has its own immediate

painting analogy / metaphor?

powers and effects – but it can also cancel, destroy, change or dissolve the meaning of, and relationships between some or all of the preceding strokes. Each of the participants has his or her own responsibility for the results.

As philosophers like Derrida and Wittgenstein have argued, the assumption that the meaning of a text or utterance is somehow immediately present, either in its words and expressions, or behind them, in the intentions of the speaker/author, is extremely problematic (see, for example, Harland, 1987; Norris, 1983, 1987). The meanings depend on the context and on the uses. In addition to this they seem to be supplementary – they depend on each other, and on whole systems of meaning. A concept of 'mouse', as contrasted with 'non-mouse' is immediately understandable only in a certain context and system of meaning. We could in different places and situations talk, for example, about 'animal companion', 'meat', 'the grey spot', 'the fur-ball', 'the nuisance' and 'Mickey' in reference to the same object. The meanings are also ambiguous in relation to time. They are all the time transformed and destabilized by what happens afterwards and what is imagined to happen in future utterances and on future lines and pages.

These issues help to make a distinction between two different approaches to texts and dialogues. The first is to study texts and utterances from the viewpoint of their immediate presence, as something with a definite identity. The second approach, strongly preferred in this book, is to look at these words and utterances in relation to the simultaneous 'traces', 'shadows' or 'haloes' of other words and utterances.

But how can we study or describe interrelated, partly unspecified and continuously changing fields of meaning? The difficulty appears analogous to that which is seen in quantum physics, where the methods of research always seem to blend with, or mess up, the objects of study. The mere attempt to examine something as unitary, excludes at least some of the indefiniteness, 'temporariness' and 'fieldness'.

uncertainty principle - the more accurately one measures the position of something the more that object is displaced

Multivoicedness: 5th café

A: It's nice up here.

B: Yes.

A: See . . . the village we are going to is there. Can you see it?

B: It looks nice . . . but everything is too tidy for my taste, lifeless in a sense.

A: It is natural because you don't yet know anybody here. Oh . . . A lager would be fine . . . and a sausage. I can pay. What do you have?

B: I still don't have any currency.

A: You can change money down there. I can pay.

B: OK.

A: You know, I have been thinking about what we talked about some time ago . . . about movement . . .

B: About the metaphor of dance?   *— establishing common ground*
                                      see pp 41

A: Yes . . . in a way also about dance. I think the central thing *sensory* really is the multivoicedness. The therapists . . . and researchers *topic* . . . and clients . . . and everybody . . . they seem to believe that they have to find *a* secret mechanism, or *a* method or *a* *+57* certain solution, or *an* image or metaphor to deconstruct . . . *maximal* it's always an '*a*' . . . a singular thing they are looking for. And *univocality* this destroys many doors to paradise. Then they analyse things in terms of this oneness. Psychology and psychiatry is full of this. *medical* And the analysis orients towards univocal answers. The answers *Health* are meant, to end questions. Now . . . when we have problems *Sciences* . . . our minds seem to kind of freeze, we become rigid. And *not a* that is what keeps the problem going. There is only one voice, *logic* one truth. 'Where id was ego must be' should be turned to *flaw!* 'Where one was, several must be'. So I agree with Barthes that *re not* the solution has the mentality of pleasure. *zy*

B: Did he say something like that? *ere*
                                    nt not
A: Not really. I just invented it. But he saw pleasure or enjoyment *living.* as genuinely revolutionary. It is the opposing force to consequentiality. The nature of pleasure is constant mobility. They are not about seeing global, singular or eternal answers. Enjoyment is a kind of flow. It is about catching glimpses of

something of interest. Always just glimpses, like soap bubbles. If they last too long, they become stale.

B: I think I can buy that. I have not read Barthes. He sounds interesting.

A: Read him. He is one of those who died too early. He was knocked down by a bus in Paris.

B: Not a very noble way to die.

A: No.

B: By the way, I would like to test you.

A: I hate tests. What is it?

B: See the picture (*points at a poster on the wall of the café; the poster represents a piece of street in the old centre of an Italian town, probably Rome, no people are visible, the sun is shining*) and tell me what you see there. I have tried these kinds of picture-tests with many people. It is kind of a post-modern Rorschach test.

A: OK. Now let's see. I see a crowd of people, celebrating in some kind of Carnivale, about to come around the corner, but they are not yet in the picture. They . . . Maybe this is enough?

B: That is strange . . . Do you know, you are strange?

A: So, it is now officially confirmed and tested. You know, this test reminded me somehow of a discussion about stuckness I had with P. I told him that our writing was not progressing too well. You know what he said?

B: No.

A: He said: 'You should think of the metaphors you are using. You should seek the root metaphors or basic metaphors in each chapter and lay them open. Once you know on the basis of which metaphors you are writing, then it becomes easier.' I tried to find out why he thought so, but he said that this was just his experience.

B: I think it was a good idea to put metaphors in the centre. I mean . . . when we think it is all facts and truths, then it becomes rigid. Like we were saying before. You are then looking for mistakes and right answers all the time. If we can stay on the fiction side, then there are more freedoms. But can you see research as a bunch of metaphors and fiction?

A: I think I can. It is the Wittgensteinian attitude. Metaphors are perspectives. Research should seek useful perspectives. Shouldn't it?

B: I think we should follow his advice.

A: Perhaps. I have been thinking more and more about this difficulty I have with writing. And I believe it is not just writing; what we have here is also a good analogy for problems and solutions generally. When I write academically, it is often really difficult . . . I don't know. I don't understand where I get this feeling of demand from. When you have a problem you just feel the same kind of demand . . .

B: But you often seem to enjoy writing?

A: When I write fiction it is different. The words just come to my head, often without any effort. So, I think maybe solutions are just . . . I don't know, this is difficult.

B: I think I see what you are pointing at.

A: When I write academic stuff I have to make it all look like I would be making conclusions all the time. A set of explanations, a set of arguments. Conclusions based on previous conclusions. The sentences have to be tightly connected . . . in a special way.

B: You mean logically connected? Orderly and logical progress?

A: Yes . . . No . . . I mean . . . people can sometimes write crazy lines and yet have a feeling that they are thinking clearly and systematically . . . like some of this French stuff, Baudrillard, Derrida, Lacan, Deleuze, Barthes. There is no progress in Barthes' *Plaisirs du texte* for example. The list of contents is alphabetical. He just jotted down topics in alphabetical order.

B: Maybe it is an internal thing . . . maybe nobody else knows when you have written in a fictive mode, or in a . . . what . . . scientific mode. Maybe only you know that?

A: I don't believe that. I have been thinking of a continuum of ways of writing. It is about different orientations to the words and sentences used in the text itself. Or rather to the gaps between them.

B: Tell me!

A: At one end we have this serious stuff, scientific writing, rule books, and so on. The words and sentences just serve a bigger purpose. They are kind of chained to each other. 'Slave words' or 'servile words' might be good expressions. The attempt is to diminish surprises and mysteries and ambiguities which could live between words and sentences. In the middle of the continuum we could have things like lists. I talk about lists which are not that hierarchical. A shopping list could be an example. The elements of list don't need to be consequential. There might even be funny differences regarding levels of abstractions, like in that story of the emperor's belongings by Borges. At the other end we could have something which I call 'pleasure writing'. The idea with this is that each gap between words or sentences is intended to be interesting or enjoyable in some sense. The idea of serving a bigger purpose is not the primary one. The words are kind of free to do what they like if that brings about enjoyment.

B: Interesting. That is an interesting way to think of these things.

A: But it is too simple. It does not include all the other things. I mean . . . it's also . . . for example . . . so much easier to write when I don't have to claim that what I write down are authentic reports of my own inner convictions and thoughts. When they could be anybody's thoughts. I don't have to sign anything on their part. I am not responsible for bad style or the mistakes in logic. It would be nice if I could pretend that I have a million personalities. As soon as I start to think that I possess my thoughts and that I am responsible for them I become rigid and start to be afraid. I am afraid that somebody can say: 'You have wrong thoughts, you made a mistake'.

you censorship again

B: It could be the imagined audience which makes all the difference. I know that I often don't want to write anything because I am too conscious of the expected result and of the opinions of the audience. I think I am writing for this or that group of people. Then I ask: is this sentence good for this audience? I am trying to find the right thing you see.

A: You seem to suffer that more than I do. For me there is always some pleasure in the act of writing. It is a challenge, like learning a language. I like to feel that my mind is working. I don't have your difficulty at all when I write fiction . . . then I am just trying to stay inspired, to have fun. It is mainly about associations, and people can have any associations they want.

B: But to whom do you write?

A: I write mainly to myself. I try to create characters and situations which interest me. It is very different compared to . . . to the responsibility of writing where the words have to do their duty. I write down what I would like to hear somebody say. It is associational stuff. And metaphorical. The two go together. Kill the metaphoricality and you have only right or wrong answers left. I think that everyday talk is more associational. In this kind of talk or writing nobody really knows what is going to happen next.

B: But that kind of stuff could also be frightening.

A: You are right. So, strongly associational stuff needs a benevolent attitude . . . as a companion.

B: But all of these things are also cultural matters. You are held responsible for your individual thoughts . . . and you don't literally want multiple personalities.

A: Yes, but I am just saying that it would be so much easier if we could think that our ideas and thoughts are not possessed by us. We could then more easily think that their digressions or contradictions or chaos or jumps are natural. If people would just think they are writers of fiction, not possessors or researchers of truths, we would have a much easier time on this planet.

B: So, we should burn all academic books?

A: No: I just mean that we should maybe only write about things which have special significance . . . personal vibrations . . . or something like that. If we don't do it everything becomes so dry . . . the texts die. And this is why I have started to hate academic writing. I seem to talk of this every day. Do I convince you?

B: Yes. You can relax.

A: Good. You know, I have been reading Atxaga's book . . . *A Cow's Memories*. It is really strange. It is really a cow's memories . . . a cow's voice . . . or should I say, two voices. She, the cow, has an internal voice too. She calls it 'Pesado' in Spanish, I think it means 'the heavy' . . . or the 'the weight'. This internal voice requires that the cow, called 'Moo', should write her memories, and she does. It is the cow-likeness of the thinking which creates the excitement. It's so foreign. Her ideas do not follow the same paths as ours . . . and that is enjoyable. Every sentence is a kind of surprise. There is a sense of the sentences enjoying talking together . . . can I say something like that? Yes . . . they don't drag their feet and just follow each other.

B: It does not sound like a very academic book . . . that is my point. Somebody must write them too. Fiction can be alive. I didn't know you read Spanish.

A: No . . . I mean no to the first point. Yes, I do, to the second. And I am quite serious. I don't believe that research can help in being monological. As long as it tries to avoid being metaphorical.

Authoritarian talk, imaginative talk

Complaints

1 *I don't like to spend time with them any more. How could I say this . . . ? I have told you this. They . . . they never touch me. I mean, verbally. I feel so lonely there . . . with them . . . I don't belong there at all. They don't play with me . . . with my words. That is very important to me . . . this kind of play . . . and they don't share a silence when the words end . . . They don't make those sighs or pauses which say that they know what you are feeling. They are always just saying the way things are – or were. These horrific pieces of advice . . . healthy and sensible ideas . . . and histories of old times. I don't want to hear them. If I say something, it is like speaking to a well without any echoes. Or attempting to play in a chamber orchestra where everybody else is watching TV. No response, or only something nice and polite: 'That's very interesting' . . . and then they go on with their stuff. They just say things which are predictable, so that everybody can see how normal they are . . . such nice people . . . such respectable friends . . . and so normal. It is like those cheap pictures. You know, those aquarelles which are sold to tourists – harbour views and the like. Everything has to be so . . . so clear . . . Everything has to clearly picture something. They abhor abstract art. There are* *no loose ideas, no risks, nothing unsafe. They always have the right things in their minds at the right times. No craziness, no dirt, no oddities, no quirks, no perversions, just pure, well-acted normality. No shifting colours, no reflections from the surfaces. It just suffocates me. It is so insulting. I cannot participate in it. There is no way to change the subject. There is no way to change the style. It's like being a poet on a soccer field when the game goes on. They don't understand that speaking could be dreaming. The room was always full of stock phrases and standard ceremonies. Everybody said things, which you could guess from the beginning. When somebody asked me something, I knew how I should have answered. During the years it became more and more difficult to say those things. It was like a big device, a big clock grinding time. The same cycles were repeating forever. I was supposed to be one of the pinions and nothing more.*

2 *Always when I drive by that new area I get depressed. What a waste of human effort. All these houses, they are exactly like they're from Siberia. And some people even like that – in the nineties. Shouldn't we make this city more human . . . not less? And it covers at least 20 hectares. It's like a huge toilet with those shiny white and blue tiles and these metal tubes. I get the feeling that I am on the wrong planet. I cannot believe that they actually built that. I cannot believe that someone can live there. It is a monument to lack of respect for anything human and living. When I see that, I try to hold my breath and think of other things. I am sure that it is made according to some theory which is actually in vogue. I am sure the architects have nice explanations for it.*

3 *I am offered a text. This text bores me. It might be said to prattle. The prattle of the text is merely that foam of language which forms by the effect of a simple need of writing. Here we are not dealing with perversions but with demand. The writer of this text employs an unweaned language: imperative, automatic, unaffectionate, a minor disaster of static. (Barthes, 1993a: 404)*

The dialogical word

Words, which have looked so solid, so innocent, have stopped being transparent conveyors of messages. It is easier and easier to see that words are actions by which pleasurable and unpleasurable realities and relationships can be created. Referential words, words in dictionaries, are 'naked corpses', as Bakhtin would say, opposed to the rich and living nature of the words used in daily contexts.

For Bakhtin, the utterance – not the sentence – is the central element of speech communication. Focusing on utterances is consistent with a strong interest in situated action and concrete events. The utterance can be seen as the place where the systematic features of language enter into contact with unique features of situations. In Bakhtin's writing the notion of utterance is linked with the concept of 'voice'. 'Voice' refers to a unique speaking person or consciousness.

Bakhtin was thoroughly critical of traditional linguistic thought. For him it was a huge mistake to consider language only as a system and from the viewpoint of abstract rules. For him utterances were not instantiations of linguistic systems, nor mechanical accumulations of units of language (words, sentences etc.). In his view an utterance is constituted from elements which are to a great extent extra-linguistic or contextual. The sentence is a unit of language, the utterance is a unit of living speech and communication. We can think of sentences as repeatable. The utterances, however, being prepared to fit unique circumstances and momentary needs, are unrepeatable – two identical utterances never mean the same thing. Utterances are always creative.

So, according to Bakhtin (and also according to Vygotsky, see Wertsch, 1991), we can separate two forms of meaning; the abstract and the contextual (or the 'sense'). Corresponding to two kinds of meaning, we can make a distinction between two kinds of understanding. Passive understanding is used when we grasp the abstract meaning of a sentence.

Acts of active understanding are more complicated. The listener must not only 'decode' the utterance (passive understanding), but also understand why everything is said in the first place. It involves the listener relating the whole utterance to his or her own interests and assumptions, to all kinds of future options and possibilities, and to the interests of others. Thus understanding an utterance actively means, in fact, preparing a response to it.

To make things even more complex, the process of active understanding is also anticipated and counted on by the speaking person. Only this makes it possible for the inter-action to continue smoothly. The speaker normally wants to introduce readings of his own words into the foreign world of the receiver. This orientation towards the future, towards addressees and towards responses, was described as 'addressivity' by Bakhtin.

Bakhtin's model of communication represents readers and the anticipated future as actually shaping the utterances being made. Thus, the utterance does not entirely belong to the speaker, it belongs to at least two people. It also does not belong entirely to the present but also to the future. Like bridges, utterances have to have both ends to exist – they are two-sided acts, the products of reciprocal relationships between speakers and listeners of present and future.

collaborative effort

We can now see that constructionist, Bakhtinian and deconstructionist views all lead to a change in our thinking about who or what controls meaning. It is apparent that words can only partially be under our control. They are always half ours, half somebody else's (Bakhtin, 1981: 293–4). Because of this, we don't live in a world where anything goes; it is already half-specified and half-finalized. What is of great interest for our purposes is the other half, the moments and regions of indeterminacy, undecidability and ambivalence.

Bakhtin tells us also that a constitutive feature of every act or utterance is its 'tone'. Tone is thus a witness to the singularity of the situation and to the particular addressivity and responsivity of the participants. It always includes an

TONE

evaluative stance. Whatever else the utterance does (refers, performs, commands, questions etc.), it also judges.

Words and discourses must conceptualize, or reach, their objects/referents in ways that are anything but simple and direct. Bakhtin compares this act to 'a ray of light entering an atmosphere already laden with other words, accents, value-judgements and experiences of the speaker and listener' (cited in Morson and Emerson, 1990: 138). The aims or intentions of the words can be imagined as a play of colours and lights on the small particles of the dust-filled atmosphere.

The complexities created by the relationship of words to the context and by the listeners' use of active understandings, creates an *internal* dialogical aspect of the word. The word is a response to many (past, present and future) contexts simultaneously; it is dialogized from *within* by many factors. For these reasons Bakhtin considered it conceptually catastrophic to examine dialogue as any kind of script, in which one piece of speech simply follows another.

From the perspective of therapy, it is useful to be conscious of one more of Bakhtin's distinctions – that between authoritative and internally persuasive discourse. When we are listening to or participating in dialogues about clients' problems we can notice the difference between authoritarian and non-authoritarian uses of language. Authoritative text and utterance – often in the form of 'the voice of problem' – enters the consciousness as an indivisible mass. It is unable to enter in dialogues to make contact with other voices. It is a form of talk which fits to transmission models of communication. Authoritative discourse cannot be represented, it is only transmitted (Wertsch, 1991: 78–9). This kind of speech allows 'no play with its borders, no gradual or flexible transitions' (Bakhtin, 1981: 343).

In contrast to authoritative discourse, the internally persuasive discourse allows dialogical interanimation. It does not remain in an isolated and static condition. The semantic structure of an internally persuasive discourse is open

meaning
abstract   contextual
            (sense)

authortative / internally persuasive

(Wertsch, 1991: 79). It invites participation and development of the themes by other persons and voices.

The distinction between authoritative and internally persuasive speech should not be exaggerated. For any text the univocal and dialogic functions can be thought of as being in dynamic tension (1991: 79).

Texts are functionally dualistic. They work both as conveyors of meaning and generators of new meaning. The first of these functions is fulfilled best when the codes of reader/listener and author/speaker coincide, when the text has a maximal univocality. The second function is based on multivoicedness. The difference between the codes of speakers and listeners (the 'misunderstanding' in Steve De Shazer's vocabulary; De Shazer, 1991) forms the essence of the text's function as a 'thinking device' (see Wertsch, 1991: 74).

Violent words: 6th café

Common ground.

A: I don't think people need any more strange or difficult theories about therapy.

B: What has hit you today?

A: It's just that I am more and more convinced that most books about these things just make things worse. After reading them people know less about how to enjoy life and how they can help others enjoy life.

B: Why?

A: They are full of all kinds of principles which should be followed and I don't think principles help. Everything is in order but the text feels dead. And the readers have to force themselves to read the stuff. And their families suffer, and they don't get up in the morning, and their sex-life finishes, and . . .

B: (*laughs*) Stop . . . I believe you.

A: I am serious with this by the way. I really don't think we can afford any dead texts any more. The same goes with therapy. Down with principles, up with fun!

B: You seem to be getting revolutionary. Should I call the KGB?

A: Not yet. I am not a real subversive yet; I am still in the planning phase.

(*Silence. A and B taste their wine.*)

B: What are you thinking about?

A: It's just . . . It's something related. I am wondering if we can really say that violent or bad dialogue . . . or violent thoughts . . . is the main thing. I mean, the thing behind people's problems. What if somebody likes clear questions and hates poems and multivocality? Maybe it's all so individual that you cannot say anything.

B: I don't think so. We just have to take it as a norm that people prefer to be unfinalized, to have some sense of mystery and possibility about themselves. Play and fun link with this, so does quiet reverie. There are some people who are not like that, I know. But there really are violent conversations in the same sense that there is physical violence. Like in interrogations . . . or in conversations in which you cannot participate in the talk without buying an awful lot of things you don't want to buy. There is talk which tries to forbid play with itself.

A: But you cannot say the talk is at fault because one person suffers and another person doesn't. In the same situation.

B: But I would say that most people suffer when they are not allowed to participate in decisions regarding what is talked about and how. That is the main thing.

A: But let's say you are in company where everybody says only nice things. Very ordered and polite conversation. And you are not like that yourself, not at all. You like obscenities and bawdy jokes and swearing a lot. You suffer if you have to speak only in polite, empty phrases. That's violence on their part . . . and on your part too. I mean, if you open your mouth. Who is violent here?

B: But it's ridiculous to speak of that as violence. What if you are the sort of person who likes punching people in the face and at a polite party they ask you not to. Are you going to tell me that their requests do you violence? That the punch and the request not to punch are the same thing?

A: No, but I think you are missing my point.

B: Perhaps, but you can't just gloss over this. 'Violence' is a problematic word here. If you use violence in terms of conversation and restriction of conversation, how do you then talk about someone being beaten up or tortured. Doesn't it take away the power of the words for the more extreme situations? Everything is violence then, and you have no words to separate polite requests from brutal beatings.

A: Yes . . . maybe . . . but that misses something too. I feel a bit beaten by you now, perhaps we should leave it.

B: So you are feeling beaten by my saying that words shouldn't be called violent. I don't know if you are really upset or just being clever to prove your point. I think I might get intoxicated by my power and insist that you sulk for a while (*smiles and pokes A in the ribs*).

A: I do feel silenced or misunderstood. I don't feel I can quite argue against what you are saying. But somehow it's a different point. Perhaps it is the point that words get asked to do different work in different contexts. Everyone knows the word 'violence' is doing different work if we use it in a police report as opposed to describing 'violent' speech. And I do feel a bit bruised when you go into this righteousness. It makes me feel more like withdrawing.

B: OK, but I think you can take it. I can see that tough streak in the middle of you. Let's go back to what you were saying.

A: It's just that in conversation everybody has to be able to participate. There has to be good faith and mutual willingness. But people don't have that if they don't believe that the interaction can be open-ended or create possibilities somehow, that they cannot find their own words. So, it might not be the text or words directly which create the violence. Perhaps I should call it restriction or diminishment. It may be lacking the belief that the interaction can be mutually rewarding. What makes it rewarding sometimes is perhaps the feeling that the person we talk to, ourselves and the conversation are unfinalizable. That it has the potential to open possibilities. That the ideas and the forms of speaking are not pre-determined.

(*Silence*)

B: Do you mind if I change topics?

A: Feel free.

B: Do you mind if I get worked up by it?

A: No.

B: You know, what really annoys me nowadays is when somebody talks about authoritarian texts using an authoritarian voice. These people don't have any sense of paradox. It seems so crazy. I'll show you a piece that has stuck in my mind:

> When we are listening to or participating in dialogues about clients' problems we can notice the difference between authoritarian and non-authoritarian uses of language. Authoritative text and utterance – often in the form of 'the voice of problem' – enters the consciousness as an indivisible mass. It is unable to enter in dialogues to make contact with other voices. It is a form of talk which fits to transmission models of communication. Authoritative discourse cannot be represented, it is only transmitted.

So what do you think?

A: I feel like I've read that somewhere lately too . . . But . . . I think you are just a perfectionist. Would you like to forbid traditional academic writing? I mean the writer makes a good point. Could you say it any better?

B: But the paradox is so obvious. Should the critique of the authoritarian language not use some other means than authoritarian language?

Imaginative words

It is possible to visualize two extreme views of human action. The first assumes that people are like machines systematically following explicit rules when they think, act and relate to each other. The rules are out there already; they just have to be applied in particular instances. The second is to see people as imagining creatures guided by a comparison of contrasting images, visualization of courses of actions, creative use of metaphors, narratives, framings and cate-gorizations (see Johnson, 1993; MacIntyre, 1981; Taylor, 1989). Both these views can be applied to psychological help.

machines   or   imagining

The latter perspective can be linked to Wittgenstein's notions of the nature of (philosophical) problems as situations when we do not know how to go on. The same view is valid also regarding other types of human problems. When stuck, people start by themselves or jointly with others to examine the options, the possible next steps. This process requires imagination[4] – imagination requires stepping outside the objective observations and actual situational limits. The responses orient towards what has happened previously, to what happens now, and to the future.

The tasks of 'good' next things/responses are indeed varied and complex: they should make it possible to go on – often meaning that they enable us to get along with others; they should (normally) maintain, or increase, the moral status of the person and others; they should also be intelligible. The combination of these tasks cannot be met by applying ready-made rules.

At this point it is useful to look more closely at the place where continuities and new directions are created in speech: at silences or breaks between utterances – 'interactive gaps' (Shotter, 1993b). This concept refers both to the progression of meaning and the contrasts between meanings. We could say that the bridging of gaps between responses and what precedes them not only produces meaning and continuity, it also creates the relationships between people.

The concept of 'interactive gap' can be related to what Bakhtin describes as 'own words' (Bakhtin, 1981: 293–4). He speaks of own words as words and expressions in which there is *more freedom* than there is with others. 'Foreign words', carriers of truth and order, are meant to be passively received and preferably obeyed. Own words seem to make more of the potential space of interactive gaps visible; foreign words seem to obscure it.

Interactive gaps are moments during which meanings can be transformed and stabilized. They can be sites where a

---

[4] It should be remembered at this point that activities like imagination or remembering do not have to be considered individual phenomena (see Middleton and Edwards, 1990); they are correlates of discourses and dialogues.

→ even in our heads /alone
we are conversing.

steady progress of argumentative meanings is guaranteed, as well as playgrounds of contrasting and mutually effacing meaning.

We could thus conceptualize parts of the workings of imagination in relation to interactional gaps. There are in most cases no automatic ways in which to respond to what has just been said. However, in everyday life people are generally not at all conscious of the great amount of creativity that is inherent in bridging the gaps.

The concept of interactive gap is useful from numerous perspectives. The idea and experience of repetition is inherent in the concept of problems. Most of the options for psychological help try to transform the repetitive and given to something changeable and 'created'. This is clearly work with interactive gaps. The concept underlines the creativity and imaginative activities of both parties and thus reminds us of the availability of options. The idea can also be used to develop exercises where therapy trainees can start to experiment with different kinds of 'refusals' to the most obvious invitations of the gap. An introduction to the exercises can be of the following type:

> If somebody asks you: 'What is the capital of France?' you don't – in most cases – have to answer: 'Paris'. And if you do, the answer can be expressed in many ways, with many tones, accompanied with many different gestures. There is even a never-ending series of ways to refuse to answer the question at all. Some of the potential answers are abrupt and impolite, but some of them can also be experienced as polite and friendly. How about: 'I thought I was the only one with that problem', or 'If you ask that of French people, many might say that Paris is not really part of France at all,' or 'Would you like to go there?', or 'Oh, I love Paris!' Each of these answers responds to different (potentially visible) threads of the question, each of them plays with different virtual strings.

Another practical application related to the idea of interactive gaps is to ask for descriptions of options in situations where people are put in the position of more or less extreme repeatability. The answers illustrate people's ability to utilize the meaning potentials of words, situations and objects.

We present some of the answers to home assignments written by participants in a recent brief therapy course. The task was to imagine that they had to spend two weeks in one room with somebody they strongly disliked, and to give some suggestions about how the situation could be made more acceptable to *both* of them. (The following shortened descriptions and ideas are collected from the papers of several participants.)

- I could try to find nice features of the person by talking about as many different things as possible.
- I could ask about everything in their life which could bring to light possible common interests.
- We could sing together.
- We could tell each other fables, narratives and children's stories.
- We could talk about travels and about the places we would like to visit.
- We could divide the room into private and common areas.
- We could agree on having certain times each day to be alone and not to talk.
- We could plan together a program of physical exercise.
- If the tension was to rise, we could try hand-wrestling, and later on real wrestling.
- We could learn to fight verbally in a way which pleased both of us.
- I could try to find from my memories the persons with whom I have had a positive relationship and who in any way resembled my fellow-prisoner.
- We could play different games and tell jokes. We could teach each other foreign languages.
- We could plan methods of escape together.
- I could analyse my feelings regarding this person very thoroughly.
- We could discuss together what we have learned so far and what we will learn in the future.

- I could think about all those things which will feel so much better when we are free again.
- I could learn to understand how his/her mental machinery works.
✓ • I could imagine that he/she is somebody else.
- We could find more and more ways to give compliments to each other.
- I could ask him/her to talk about their problems – I could then develop compassion towards them.
- We could learn to meditate together – as an alternative to talking together.
- I could ask him/her to massage my neck – I always like anyone who does that.
- We could intentionally argue about controversial moral issues regarding which our opinions clearly differ with the goal of enhancing our skills of argumentation and tolerance.
✗/• We could change the language we speak.
- We could start to write a book about the situation.
- I could systematically start to test my words and their effects on the other person with the intention of finding those which make our interaction better.
- We could sing Christmas carols (specially effective when it's not Christmas time).
- We could tell each other about all of our wishes for the future.
- We could teach each other all the children's songs and plays we can.
- We could start a common story. The first one writes first, the other one continues.
- We could think what we will say afterwards to all the people we know. Next we could try to explain to each other the differences in things we will say.
- We would have a dance session each day: we would teach each other all the dances we can.
- We could agree that each day we will find at least one new positive thing in the other person, and then say it to them.

4

Processes of Re-enchantment

This is to say that the art of living has no history: it does not evolve: the pleasure which vanishes for good, there is no substitute for it. Other pleasures come, which replace nothing. No progress in pleasures, nothing but mutations. (Barthes, 1993b: 416)

Social poetics

Swallows' teachings: 7th café

A: Would you like me to read a bit of my presentation?

B: Why not. Is that for the congress? You've done it already?

A: It was fast: 3–4 hours. I am fast when I can do things I like, very slow with other things. You know, I am planning to find a CD or tape with bird song to start the presentation. Perhaps you could imitate some bird songs.

B: No. You said this is just a part?

A: Yes, it's about half. I am still working on the rest.

> For me swallows are birds of freedom, of warmth, of stone and of love. They simply are.
> I have had two strong experiences which relate to birds. Both of them happened in Spain on the same trip. I was 16 or 17 years old. It was my first trip to Mediterranean countries. It was one of the first years of Inter-rail. The train arrived in Spain and stopped in Gerona, north of Barcelona. It was a very warm night in June. We could see some old buildings. But what dominated the experience were the swallows, my favourite birds. I just like them. I especially like their twittering or chirping. I like some other birds too. My second favourite birds are canaries. I especially like their twittering or chirping. I like it even more in a city when the sounds echo from walls. There were

hundreds of them flying in all directions. The combined effect of a warm Mediterranean summer-evening, an old city with buildings made of light stone materials, the swallows, the sounds, was inexplicably powerful. It was also very homely. I felt like being back in my real home.

I like to talk about this topic. It is a good topic for me. Warm nights, swallows, light stone. After the Gerona-phenomenon I have often thought of writing something, a poem maybe, of this experience. I often felt that it somehow requires expression. I made some attempts – I often get poetic bouts when I have a couple of glasses of wine. Languages are my hobby so I sometimes try to write in other languages.

Last winter we had a workshop in Salamanca. Salamanca, a Spanish city, is definitely a good town for swallows. I could see that even in the winter. It is also a town where it can get very hot in summer – and a town of light stone . . . *ciudad de piedra dorada*. You can guess the rest: I had to write a poem about swallows, and warmth, and stone. And I did it too. The words of this piece of text – I am not reading it – were quite special for me. These kind of words are good words for me.

I have a theory of psychological problems. It does not explain all problems, but perhaps many of them. The theory goes like this: problems relate to the use of words which do not resonate for the person or persons if there are many people involved. Using these kinds of words is not good. They create emptiness, they create deserts, they create violence. Therapists should avoid talk which encourages the use of foreign, empty, non-resonating words. The concept 'word' here is used more or less metaphorically to refer to sentences, expressions, individual words, stories etc. This is the end of the first theoretical part.

* * *

The image we generally have of helping, of rehabilitation, or of psychotherapy, is that in these areas we are, or should be, talking of facts and real issues, of business, so to speak. We teach professionals techniques of how to conduct interviews, how to get relevant information.

But what if this is all wrong? What if the best way is to look for living words and expressions? How should we teach then? How should we do therapy? How are powerful words found, how is resonance found? Is there a swallows' way to talk? Can swallows speak of rehabilitation – would they?

To me the language of psychotherapy, psychiatry, psychology and rehabilitation is almost a total wasteland. For me these are names for collections of dead words, dead gestures. They are masses of words which only seldom, and with a great difficulty, can be made to caress or to have music. They have some powers left, a power to scare perhaps. There could be a glimpse of divinity: the promise of telling about the deepest secrets of the soul, about mysteries of creativity etc. There is also an 'Alice in Wonderland' quality in many of the models and expressions.

I would like to put up signposts and warnings around these languages. The signs could say: 'Beware of dangerous words . . . these words can harm you.' They look so harmless, most of them, but like vampires, they can drain your blood and transform you into a zombie.

Children know a lot more than most adults about how to make resonating words, singing words, sad words, joyful words. Some authors are also better than others at keeping words alive. One of my favourites is Bernardo Atxaga, a Basque writer. In the book *Obabakoak* he tells criss-crossing stories, some realistic, some mythical, about a village with the same name. The protagonists change constantly and appear in each other's stories. In *Dos Hermanos,* he talks about two adolescent brothers who are guarded and protected by animals – squirrels, a snake and different types of birds. The story is told through the voices of these animals (there is also a chapter told by a star). In *Memorias de una vaca* (A Cow's Memories) the voice is that of a cow who does not want to be a regular, stupid cow – she thinks that there is nothing more stupid than a stupid cow. In all these books the author succeeds in creating characters that produce very interesting and inspiring words. Have you ever heard how a cow thinks, or a squirrel? If you haven't – you can read the book.

* * *

I have many good memories of a childhood in a city. The best of them are quite abstract, they link with colours, smells and hard-to-describe sensations and atmospheres. One of the most beautiful of them relates to the sun of a summer afternoon at home in the yard. My family lived then in a part of town where almost all the houses are made of red brick. In this memory there is a combination of children's voices playing in the yard, the warmth, the tanned skins of children, sunny walls, the smells of stone, of certain small city plants, of asphalt. Another set of memories is connected to blue sky and sea. And not only a real sea but a pretend sea. I remember how we used to play a certain board game with one of my childhood friends. The colour of the sea on the playing board was exactly the colour of the blue sea. I remember the beauty of the game, even the names of some of the places were beautifully exciting then, like Valparaiso.

This friend died in an accident a couple of years ago. And I have seldom felt such a loss, even though we did not have anything to do with each other after school years. When I remember him, I always remember the games we played and the colours of the room, the green pile carpet (which was often a forest in the games), the blue sky visible from the window, the sun in the room. This boy was such a source to beauty, how could a person like this die?

B: Let me interrupt for a minute. I was drifting with my own associations, and I don't know if I should move from the feeling of what you were saying, but I was struck when you said your friend was a 'source to beauty'. I don't know if that was a mistake you read or a deliberate use of words that is quite profound. The usual phrase is a 'source of beauty', of course. A 'source to beauty' says something else, quite different.

A: Yes . . . I don't know . . . I'll go on perhaps and we can come back to it.

Most people like the fact that other people like something, even if they don't like the things the others like. To demonstrate this I shall read aloud a piece of somebody's likes (it is Roland Barthes):

J'aime, je n'aime pas
I like: salad, cinnamon, cheese, pimento, marzipan, the smell of new cut hay (why doesn't somebody with a nose make such a perfume?), roses, peonies, lavender, champagne, loosely held political convictions, Glenn Gould, too cold beer, flat pillows, toast, havana cigars, Händel, slow walks, pears, white peaches, cherries, colours, watches, all kinds of writing pens, desserts, un-refined salt, realistic novels, the piano, coffee, Pollock, Twombly, all romantic music, Sartre, Brecht, Verne, Fourier, Eisenstein, trains, Medoc wine, having change, Bouvard and Pecuchet, walking in sandals on the lanes of southwest France, the bend of Adour seen from doctor L's house, the Marx Brothers, the mountains at seven in the morning leaving Salamanca . . . (Barthes, 1993b: 417–18)

So, a conclusion. Bluntly: I think we should be suspicious of official talk, neutral talk, nobody's talk, and talk more of what people like, of what enchants them, of what inspires them – and less about what they don't like. This would be useful, helpful and fun. It would also be better rehabilitation and psychotherapy than most rehabilitation and psychotherapy today. So I think we should give voice back to many things, also to words.

This is what I liked to say. These words were friendly ones today. There were some words which would have been eager to present themselves but I could not include them today. I am sorry for that. Maybe some other time. I am sure it will come.

A: So did you like it?

B: Yes . . . yes.

A: You sound hesitant.

B: I don't know . . . It is so jumpy . . . but I like the quirkiness. And it is also quite personal, quite you. And the bird songs. That is nicely crazy.

A: Any critique?

B: Yes, I think I am being too polite again. Everything is 'words', I think you maybe take the metaphor too far and almost lose sight of it being a metaphor. I worry a bit that you might do it to death.

A: How?

B: Sometimes I was thinking . . . 'Why is he using the word 'word' here?' It sounds so . . . so trivial in a sense.

A: But you must know that I used it in the Bakhtinian sense . . . and it is about the powers of words in a relational sense. So how could it be misunderstood? It's about finding these kinds of ideas and perspectives and words together. I think that this could be the main thing . . . to find these overlapping resonances and use them. And it is also about taking ourselves, our experiences, our personal meanings seriously. How can we take a client's experiences seriously if we don't take our own ones seriously? How can we take the shared experiences seriously if we are not sensitive to experience in the first place?

B: I understand . . . I understand. Take it easy. Your presentation is also very non-academic. It is about your own interests. People are supposed not to talk of them. It is a difficult topic for many. You are not supposed to say that 'I am important . . . my experiences matter . . . you should listen to me . . . you should be interested in my likes'. I am interested in your likes but I still think some people would say 'Why should I care what he likes?' or even feel resentful, 'Why should I have to listen to him indulging himself?', and 'Why is he in a position to indulge himself, no one seems to care what I like?'.

A: I know. But I generally like the likes of others, I think they are interesting, much more interesting than complaints anyway. I enjoy the presence of pleasure. I think everybody does. Don't you?

B: Perhaps, but some other people's pleasures are annoying. Part of me doesn't care what Barthes likes. I think, 'He likes havana cigars'; I hate cigars – what if he smokes it next to me? Part of me thinks 'What gives him the right to like cigars?'.

A: What gives you the right to like cappuccino?

B: Cappuccinos are different . . . anyway I'll give them up . . . (*laughs*). There is something about assuming a power to speak of these things . . . about who has the privilege to speak of these things and who doesn't . . . but if some people are silenced I know it doesn't help for me to take up wearing sackcloth and ashes . . .

A: I think they would suit you . . . you have a strange confusion of social justice and catholic guilt.

B: But you say things which relate to empowerment and justice and then lose it. You always end up with everything seeming to come back to pleasure and fun. I think meaning, mystery, possibility, dignity, the right to self-definition are all implied somehow, but seem to get dropped out of the conclusions.

A: Yes, of course, but I think this pleasure stuff is linked with all of that. It is just so difficult to talk of these things. We cannot continue this crazy, academic, psychological stuff and deny our own interests and pleasures – it is madness. We have to acknowledge the importance of finding pleasure in talking with people and being together with people. I don't believe that good results or solutions come from misery. The old prioritizing of pain, the endless focus on misery and times of sacrifice, this S–M stuff is over. At least for me. I might have to leave academia because of this.

B: What do you do then?

A: I'll become a writer.

Metaphors, perspectives, social poetics: 8th café

A: I am not sure if I like the word 'metaphor'. It reminds me of the fact that people are still quite seriously arguing about meanings being metaphoric or literary.

B: Do you have a better suggestion?

A: I think I have. Perspective. Talk is always perspectival or positional. Nobody is really claiming it isn't. Except the objectivists and realists, and who would believe them any-more? Talk makes some relationships, connections, positions and differences visible. This is also true for metaphors . . . they make these kinds of things visible. Therapy is also about making new things visible.

B: No metaphors, just perspectives? Is that what you are saying?

A: Yes.

B: So what?

A: One thing is that we should also see the concept of 'meta-phor' perspectivally. There are many metaphors for metaphor . . . I mean, many ways to describe perspectivality, or seeing something as something. The main thing is really that there is some freedom of choosing what this 'as if' might be. Metaphor is just one word which refers to the experience of seeing things 'as if' they were something.

B: I am not sure if I get your point.

A: Let's try some examples. You wake after a dream and still see your surroundings to some extent through it. So the dream creates an 'as if'. If you are hungry you see a hamburger as edible, if not, it appears greasy and smelly. If you are trying to sell a car you see people as potential buyers.

B: I recently saw a dance performance where an image of another person was projected on the dancer. So there were kind of two faces . . . or three. The third face was really not the projected one, nor the real one. It was really interesting and also scary.

A: There was something like that also in an art exhibition recently. There was a talking head projected on to a flower, a bruised face projected on a pillow under a chair, and so on. But the main thing is, I think, that there is a sense of deepness of things not being only one thing. You can get this sense of deepness in many ways. If you know a secret about something, if you see something through nostalgic eyes, if you have a mythical frame of mind, if you play.

B: You are saying that we can lose this deepness and that losing it can cause trouble and that it would be good to regain it?

A: Yes. Because the return of metaphors . . . of superimposed images or realities . . . creates possibilities for seeing and experiencing things in richer ways.

B: You know, I think you have a problem there.

A: What is it?

B: I think 'metaphors' are more than 'perspectives'. They imply a grasp of several realities simultaneously. They cannot be about one reality. 'Perspective' is a poorer concept.

A: Yes . . . you have a point.

B: 'Perspective' fits with those cognitive ideas of reframing and re-thinking. For a long time now I have felt that they are quite limiting.

A: How do you see them as limiting?

B: It is difficult to connect them to sociality and things like play. What we have been talking about recently is something else. It has to do with . . . I cannot find a good word. The word Shotter uses nowadays . . . 'social poetics'. That captures things better. There can be no social poetics without metaphoricality of language . . . or of gestures . . . or something. And the word 'perspective' does not really connect well with ideas like sacred.

A: 'There can be no social poetics without metaphoricality of language or gestures.' It's a little cumbersome but that is a nice phrase, really nice.

Contexts of the sacred

A house

Maison, pan de prairie, ô lumiere de soir
Soudain vous acquèrez presque un face humaine
Vous êtes près de nous, embrassants, embrassés.

(House, patch of meadow, oh evening light
Suddenly you acquire an almost human face
You are very near us, embracing and embraced.)

Rainer Maria Rilke,
in Bachelard (1994: 8)

Two dreams

1   *'I remember once having a dream about spaceships. I was looking from the window and there were innumerable space-ships in the sky. They were all shapes and colours. Some looked like the UFOs in TV series, some had absolutely fantastic shapes. They were totally noiseless and just glided on the sky. There were thousands of them; the whole sky was covered by them. The strangest thing was that nobody else minded them. They seemed to notice them but they did not have any impact. I was just astonished because of this lack of admiration. When I woke up I felt both frightened and grateful because of the dream. There was a very strong sense of message.'*

2   *'I was in a small town near my home. There was a big field quite close to the town. On the field there were many animals, some of them mythical. I especially remember the "ligon", a mixture of a tiger and a lion. Near the town I could see a big eland, with huge horns curving slightly backwards. In a way I knew that I was those animals. After awakening I thought that they were kinds of powers to which I usually don't have a connection.'*

Positive deep: 9th café

A: Have you seen the film *Hook*? There were some wonderful things in it.

B: No, but I saw *Peter Pan*.

A: It's almost the same thing. There was a wonderful scene in *Hook* when the 'Lost Boys' tried to teach Peter Banning . . . who had forgotten that he is actually the grown-up Peter Pan

... to fly again. They said to him: 'Only one happy thought ... think one happy thought and you can fly.' It took him some time, but he learned ... I think that is nicely put ... 'one happy thought'.

B: So you come back to the old topic ... pleasure talk. Do I really get you right ... you sincerely do believe that the main thing is to introduce something you call pleasure talk, don't you? It sounds so wonderfully trivial. But nobody buys that ... it's not academic enough ... you should talk of instincts or Foucault, discourses, difference of '*jouissance*' and '*plaisir*', and signs and simulation ... that's much better ... And what about other people? It sounds so individualistic.

A: Yes ... I agree ... in a sense what I am saying is trivial, but I don't mean it *that* trivially. I think we should have social perspectives on this too. It is not at all a purely individual thing I am talking about. Even the happy thoughts in the *Hook* film were kind of shared joys. And besides, I don't think it is so easy to think these kinds of happy thoughts. For Peter Banning it was excruciatingly difficult at that moment. I just ... sometimes it is very difficult to get people to talk about what they like. I think this links with the stuff about approach and avoidance orientations.

B: Explain! Please ...

A: How would I start ... ? It's ... no ... I read a book some years ago. I think it was Tinbergen, a German ... there was something about the behavioural modes of animals ... the approach mode and the avoidance mode. All of this stuff comes from ethology. They are very different things these two. If you think there is a threat, you are very interested in what everything *really* is. To prepare yourself for an attack, you have to locate the enemy, you have to *know* how things are. If you are having fun, you don't mind. You can look at things and let your mind wander around and play with whatever pleases it ... in a sense. But that demands safety. Safety is the foundation for play, in a way.

B: I get your point.

A: But the main thing is that these two orientations have a very different orientation to 'deepness' ... to multiple realities. When you are afraid about what is really happening under the smooth surface of things. It is kind of . . . paranoid depth. Things are not as they seem to be and it is bad. The whole approach is more logical, more rational. People try to stick to some definite truths and ideas about negative possibilities and then build their fortresses against certain kinds of enemies. Approach mode is different. The interest is more . . . more fluid. There is no need to build fixed theories. The depth is . . . it is about pleasant possibilities under the surface . . . about dreaming. Fear and daydreams are very different.

B: I see what you are pointing at, but 'pleasant' is a misleading word here. You don't just mean having fun.

A: No, the depth is often about meaningfulness and dignity, a sense of recognition of other aspects of ourselves, or recognition of unspoken but valued motivations . . . It relates to the idea of providence and sacredness in a way.

B: That takes it much further. I feel I have a glimpse of what you mean, but I'm not clear.

A: This approach kind of depth can be gained in many ways. One is rituals. In them things are not what they seem to be. And think of play . . . And art . . . maybe art is a good example? Art tells us that reality is not simple and flat . . . that you can see many things in almost anything . . . Or being in love. When you are in love, you see wonderful things happening in the everyday life which was so dull a week ago. So this is what I think happens in therapy when it works, it introduces multiple meanings or deepness to places where there was only certainty before. And this can happen in many ways.

B: But you cannot mean that it helps just to talk about whatever . . . whatever nice things?

A: That too can often be very useful . . . I am sure. But what I have in mind is different. Should I tell you or shouldn't I?

B: Why this secrecy? Tell me, share your wisdom.

A: I think that is a good example, irony. As soon as you say 'share your wisdom' I know your words are not what they seem. You certainly don't think I am so wise.

B: I do. How could you doubt it?

A: No you don't. But anyway . . . And one thing is humour. Whatever creates a feeling of depth . . . of positive depth –

that's important . . . 'positive depth'. It would be a good term, a good name for an article or a book.

B: So, what's the difference between positive deep and negative deep?

A: I am not sure about that . . . it could be partly just that . . . that the positive deep is not too unpredictable. There has to be an atmosphere of trust, basic trust. You know, what disturbs me in this respect are these psychological models of control and life-control, you know . . . locus of control, outcome expectancy.

B: What do they have to do with this?

A: They imply . . . they have a funny picture of pleasure. They kind of combine control and pleasure. I admit that they have something in common . . . I mean, of course you have to be relatively secure to enjoy. But they seem to forget that pleasure is also revolutionary . . . Because it creates indifference it is an antidote to oppressive knowledges.

B: Indifference, in what sense?

A: Indifference to knowing for certain, for knowing for ever. And therapy is about finding things which connect to the positive deep, to pleasure in the areas of life which are problematic. In this way people will get antidotes to oppressive forms of interaction which problems represent. No . . . which problems are. All this can happen in many ways . . . People often forget that they have to constantly find these positive deeps, alone and together. So, in this sense I really see pleasure as the cure.

B: Comes quite close to individualist, old-fashioned positive thinking?

A: I don't see it like that. The pleasure may be at finding new possibilities of meaning, that dignify an impossible situation, not denying the external situation. And positive thinking is not the best way anyway, it tends to impose a formula. I think I am referring more to listening carefully, listening together. We have to listen to signs of promise in the atmosphere, in the voices, in the bodies. Together and alone.

B: Is that all?

A: No. And when we hear and feel the promise, we must act accordingly. And then do the same thing again. And again.

B: Sounds heavy.

A: No, it's the easiest thing in the world.

Shared responsibility for providence: 10th café

A: I think that I now understand something more about topics.

B: Tell me if you do. For me the whole thing is quite hazy.

A: For me too, but I now understand better why the matter is so confusing. And if we think of therapy in Vico's or Bakhtin's terms, it is clear that topics are not chosen. The word is more or less a synonym for 'situation' or 'atmosphere'. Actually I think it is also a way of looking at emotions, a rather strange way. Atmosphere might be the best word here. But Bakhtin's viewing of the 'situation' is so dynamic that it is hard to find good ways to talk about it. The other difficulty is that this perspective in relation to topics is in strong contrast to the more common uses. The usual use is to see the topic as something which can be chosen. This easily mixes things up.

B: This much I understand.

A: I also think that Bakhtin himself moved along a continuum of concreteness and dynamism regarding the concept.

B: What do you mean?

A: The structure of language makes us talk about situations as active or agentive . . . like . . . 'my back is killing me' . . . 'the scenery soothes my nerves' . . . 'I like the atmosphere tonight'. We are reacting to them like they were persons, or something like persons. But mostly Bakhtin is talking of something more complex. Sometimes he seems to imply that the concept refers to past things . . . that the topics are formed by the things which previously happened, or which have been talked about. On the other hand he talks of the topic as the 'living context' and in this connection he refers to anticipations and things like that.

B: That starts to be quite difficult . . . but it still makes some sense.

A: But there is much more to it.

B: Beware of wrecking my old and only brain!

A: One of the really difficult ones is the 'topic' in relation to evaluation. Bakhtin sees topics as moral evaluators in a way.

The situations and contexts we are in and reacting to all have their moral perspectives and implications. His topics are not morally innocent.

B: I get that. But what are the practical conclusions of this view . . . are there some?

A: I think there are many of them. They have to do with emotions and promise and responsibility, with all the things we have been talking about . . . in many different ways.

B: They are not very obvious.

A: Perhaps not. I think it is easier if we start from the word 'atmosphere'. It is easy to see that individual people can have lots of influence regarding things like that. It is also evident that atmospheres, I mean social or emotional atmospheres, invitations of the moments, they are not *only* about what individuals do. They are more than that. And whatever people do when they react to the felt invitations of the moment . . . changes them. People cannot not participate in developing these atmospheres. So, there are individual responsibilities and group responsibilities here.

B: Group responsibilities? In what sense?

A: People have to commit themselves to create good moments, dialogues and atmospheres. They have common responsibilities for the dialogue and for the interaction. Like in sports. The whole team works for the goals. It relates partly to accountability, to trust . . . to things like that, but not only to them.

B: I see. But how does all this fit to the ideas about metaphors and things like that. I have struggled with understanding how to make that link.

A: I think it is quite a complex link. And sincerely don't think anybody can say too much about it. Maybe the poets can. I don't know. But I think I understand bits and pieces of it. It has to do with those things we said about the difficult and easy forms of writing, you remember?

B: Yes. The violent and the pleasurable, the convincing style and the momentary style.

A: It has something to do with all the stuff about 'good stories' Jerome Bruner and others have been talking about. Some ways of writing and talking make it easier for the readers and audiences to participate and to identify with the characters. And think of all those symbols around which people gather . . . flags . . . football teams . . . rock idols . . . symbols of life styles. But not anything will do. I think that people tend to gather around symbols which are somehow still alive for them. They can gain a sense of deepness and meaningfullness from them. The sense of promise is connected to this because the sense of deepness has a lot to do with opening up . . . opening of possibilities. There are new possibilities because there are kind of . . . because the reality is not one-dimensional any more. We can be trapped only in that kind of a reality.

B: I don't see so much new there.

A: Maybe not. It is just one of those things which has to do with responsibilities of participants I was talking to.

B: I lost your point.

A: I think the participants of dialogues have a shared responsibility to seek and produce these living or enlivening things, whatever they are . . . symbols, metaphors, myths, topics. I mean they have to resonate for all of them, at least to some extent. I don't know how this type responsibility should be called. 'Responsibility for shared promise and resonance'?

B: Responsibility for the sacred? For the providence?

A: Perhaps. That sounds good. 'Shared responsibility for providence'.

A suburban kitchen: 11th café

A: Can I read you a piece I just wrote? We could then talk about it?

B: Please.

A: It goes like this:

> A friend has complained about his apartment and kitchen for years. The kitchen is modern. All the cupboards and equipment are of a standard type. He complains that it disturbs him to think that all the other apartments in this building and also in the neighbouring buildings, must have something similar. Everything is light coloured. The doors, walls, cupboards, refrigerators, ovens, floors, ceilings, are all creamy white. You often hear the refrigerator's small buzzing

sound in the background. The man says that he is ashamed of the apartment and kitchen, both of them feel undignifying and cheap. For him it is easy to feel like an unsuccessful person in his home. He wonders if it is because the furniture, doors and all the other modern objects seem to be purely functional – they appear to refer only to themselves and to their own purpose. The white walls and doors are made to cover the plates, kettles, spoons, forks and foodstuffs, to be easily washable – and also easy (and cheap) to make? Or could it be because the whole thing is so thoroughly and so successfully preplanned – perhaps the style is too uniform?

* * *

A: That was it. What do you think?

B: In what sense?

A: I mean . . . is there something lacking in the kitchen or is it just a lack of something . . . imagination perhaps . . . creativity.

B: I think it is both. That there really are depriving places and objects and that sometimes people lack creativity.

A: After this trip to Indonesia I have been thinking more and more about the balance of nature and our cities. Somehow nature feels more of an underdog here. I talked of this with two architects recently. It seems to me that people no longer notice how important it is to have something referring to the spiritual sphere in buildings and cities.

B: Spiritual? What is in opposition to spiritual then?

A: Functionalism. I believe that functionalism is harmful because it forgets the need for the spiritual. The architect from Iceland seemed to agree, she said that in her culture people still have lots of respect for spirits of nature – she has this herself. The Finnish architect seemed not to understand my point at all. I think buildings should be somehow . . . subordinate to nature . . . less important than them and less important than people . . . Now they are kind of insults to nature and its shapes.

B: I see what you mean. I have been thinking that we should put much more effort into finding stories or myths which bring the sacred or spiritual back. They should maybe be pagan myths because Christianity so often tends to be taken as anti-sensual and very much a one-truth religion.

A: That reminds me. I read recently a story of Antonio Tabucchi – *Requiem* – where he pays his respect to the Portuguese poet

Fernando Pessoa. The book is about wandering in an almost empty Lisbon on a very hot Sunday in July and meeting figures . . . or rather spirits . . . which have something to do with Pessoa. There is absolutely no division between dreams and what is real in that book . . . that is why I liked it. I think it would be a real cultural achievement to write those kinds of books for other cities.

B: You know this French sociologist, Maffesoli, talks about these kinds of things . . . The main point seems to be that modern societies, modern in the sociological sense . . . believers in progress, in postponing enjoyment, and so on . . . have tried to separate dreams and reality. In fact, he says that this is the central mechanism of power, to make people forget dreams. He also talks of a re-enchantment which he thinks is happening now. People do not believe in cold rationalism as much anymore; it is rapidly losing credibility. What is gaining stature is privileging being together. Images and totems of all kind are replacing abstract ideas and arguments. It is easy to gather around images and symbols. Their effects are more immediate.

A: Interesting.

B: Maffesoli also makes an interesting distinction between Apollonian and Dionysian orientations. Dionysus was attached to earth and its pleasures, to sharing together; Apollo lived in the sky, he was a guy of clear views and principles.

A: I think it was Swinburne who said: 'Is not Apollo a beautiful god to behold, a terrible god to follow.'

B: True.

Towards a sense of the sacred in dialogue

Sacred can have many meanings, but at least in part, being sacred means being outside total (human) control and understanding. Anthropologists claim that the sacred objects and scenes have a similar nature and special place in all cultures. Their function is to connect the profane world to that of divinities. They are the means by which humans can in some way participate in the sacred. For the objects to keep their powers, people have to believe that they have some properties which do not belong to a world under human control.

Sacredness can be a prerequisite of curiosity and desire. Desire is not a matter of knowing already, it is the product of the interplay of the familiar and the unknown. There can be no desire if the mystery has disappeared, if everything is known and under control.

We will examine questions related to sacred through the concepts of 'myth', 'play' and through Bakhtin's ideas about the 'topic' or living context.

Myths are stories of times and places where gods and people meet. They are located at liminal moments of history and at liminal places. At these moments and places people stop being powerless, they acquire some of the powers of gods, still retaining some of the weaknesses of humans (for example, Serres, 1993). Similarly, the gods transforming or giving birth to humans still retain some of their powers and acquire some of the weaknesses of people. In many religions, the liminal space is inhabited by intermediary half-god-like, half-human figures, angels and tricksters (Eliade, 1991; Serres, 1993). These creatures can be messengers for both humans and gods; they also have some of the powers of gods.

For these reasons myths have a special place in maintaining tension between the known and not-known. They lead us to see that things are 'deeper' than they look. Dual meanings and 'deepness' are, of course, also produced by science and by virtually any interpretations involving things 'under the surface'. The 'sense of deepness' produced by science is, however, of a much more limited kind.

Mircea Eliade tells us that one of the main features of ancient cultures, and also of many 'primitive cultures' of today, is that almost everything happening is seen as related to, or as a repetition of, old myths or creation stories (Eliade, 1991). Because experiences, actions and happenings are contrasted with the actions of mythical figures they have multiple meanings. A fisherman leaving the harbour in the morning or a hunter following the game is not only fulfilling a prosaic task, he is also repeating the action of a mythical hero. Children playing with each other give good illustrations of this process; their play involves constant negotiation of how to connect to images which have a mythical character.

There are also other perspectives to the sacred: Bataille spoke about the indirect or residual nature of 'inner experience', which in his vocabulary was closely related to the experience of personal sovereignty and worth. The starting point in his thought was that people naturally abhor being univocally defined or being returned to a state of factuality, of the totally known (or 'the homogenised' to use Bataille's own expression). There is no experienced sovereignty or feeling of freedom in being totally described and emptied by words.

Play resembles myths because of its inherent duality. Play is always play with levels of reality. There is always something which must be assumed to really exist (toys, playground, playmates, rules of play) for play to become possible. Play does thus not signify stepping out of reality – it means being flexible with realities. It is about being able to experiment with different relationships. What the players are relating to is changed: for a child a carpet can become an ocean; for believers a cup can be a chalice.

In Western hierarchies of values play is usually seen as something secondary, as something luxurious. It would, however, be possible to invert the hierarchy and see play as primary and reality as a derivative, perhaps as frozen play.

One important thing common to things like play, art and myths is that they can give us a sense of power we 'normally' don't have (or don't see that we have). Touched by them, the world is no longer only what it seems to be, it becomes a plenitude. The meaning of repeating trivial things, even the meaning of suffering, can change.

On this basis we can suggest one more metaphorical understanding of the process of change in successful therapies: we could think that people just learn again to play with something which has been unplayable. Problems are, from this perspective, districts of experiential one-dimensionality, areas of not-play, domains of non-pleasure, regions of imposed truth. 'Solutions' can correspondingly be anything which introduces play, pleasure or a sense of the sacred. The change could also be described as the development of 'poetic' relationships to those words and stories defining previously problematic areas of one's identity and life.

Some of Bakhtin's ideas about conceptualizing conversational processes can be helpful in this context by illuminating how dialogues could be effective in transforming one-dimensional interaction and experience to multi-dimensional.

One interesting feature of Bakhtin's thought is his way of talking about the context of speech as 'living'. For Bakhtin there are at least three persons, or person-like factors, involved in all speech, even in monologues. All three factors are shaping every utterance of a speaking person. Two of these factors belong (at least partly) to the speaker: (i) their own intentions of saying or achieving something and (ii) their orientation towards the addressee (the perspectives, motives and position of the addressee have to be taken into account and anticipated in forming the utterance).

Utterances, however, are also shaped by the *previous* utterances, by the 'already-spoken-about'. This third factor, constitutive of every utterance, was described by Bakhtin as a 'topic'. He talked about it in different ways at different points of his career. One understanding of topic was referred to by a cryptic expression, the 'hero', which we suggest may be considered as 'central protagonist' or 'key person'. Another description, perhaps the most appropriate one for our purposes, was the 'living context' within which, or in response to which, a conversation occurs. A third concept belonging to the same family was the 'super-addressee'. The 'superaddressee', he suggested, was constitutive of our conversations – a sense that someone would understand what we were saying, even if our interlocutor at that moment did not.

speech
1) intention
2) orient w/ addressee
3) topic

SUPER ADDRESSEE

While two sides of the speaker's voice orientate towards the goals and the listener, the third side is turned towards a virtual, always somewhat ambiguous and uncontrollable[1] 'third person' (the 'situation', 'the already happened/ talked about', the 'living context', the 'hero', the 'superaddressee') with which the participants are always in relationship. This relationship is the central source of sense of promise as well as hopelessness. We are not talking about something personified in the sense of 'God' or 'Science', but of a metalinguistic factor constitutive of *all* utterances.[2] The 'topic' or 'situation' always contributes to the tone, shape and meaning of what we say. It is human-like in a special sense: we have to take it into account in the same way we would take into account other people. It does not speak to us, but we behave and speak as if it did. We could also say that this phenomenon, which often goes unnoticed, introduces an element of sacredness to every interaction. Noticing it means being open to one's own and other's emotions and to the special atmospheres, invitations and sensibilities of the moment.

Interaction, talk and internal dialogues cannot help continuously producing ever-changing 'topics'. They are something which temporarily 'holds' people – something which organizes the interactions, relationships and experiences. Whatever topic/scenes are, we are always in a relationship with them. We act and talk 'into' the possibilities and temptations of the 'situation' as we see it. We do things to transform 'it'.

The limits and definitions of topics can be disputed at any moment – there are no objective limits. Each attempt to talk about them or control them ends in changing them – topics in the Bakhtinian sense are correlates of all interaction. This does not prevent people experiencing continuity of topics: a

---

[1] It is ambiguous and uncontrollable because it is a product not of individual intentions and plans but of 'joint action', which can never be totally controlled by one person (see Shotter, 1993a).

[2] One implication of Bakhtin's views is that we are always in a *social* situation, even when we are totally alone.

Semantic associations – 'bridges' alter topic

depressed person can feel that his or her whole life is one long tragedy with the same drab scene going on forever. For a child each moment can bring a new world.

It is impossible to define at what exact moment and to what measure a topic is shared by the participants. It is equally difficult to define when it turns to another. It is important to notice that the notion of therapy depends on the human capability of *jointly* having *some* control of topics – but much of the transformation of topics is outside the power of our manipulations.

All topics support some connections, orientations, roles and moral positions at the expense of others. Some of them can trigger a downward spiral of hate, others can create an upward abyss called 'love'.

very dualistic
only 2 ways to go ↗up
↘down

5

Metaphors of Therapy and Good Interaction

Interacting well

No packaged words

Belisa Crepusculario had been born into a family so poor they did not even have names to give their children. She came into the world and grew up in an inhospitable land where some years the rains became avalanches of water that bore everything away before them and others when not a drop fell from the sky and the sun swelled to fill the horizon and the world became a desert. Until she was twelve, Belisa had no occupation or virtue other than having withstood the hunger and the exhaustion of centuries. During one interminable drought, it fell to her to bury four younger brothers and sisters; when she realized that her turn was next, she decided to set out across the plains in the direction of the sea, in hopes that she might trick death along the way . . .

Belisa Crepusculario saved her life and in the process accidentally discovered writing. In a village near the coast, the wind blew a page of newspaper at her feet. She picked up the brittle yellow paper and stood a long while looking at it, unable to determine its purpose, until curiosity overcame her shyness. She walked over to a man who was washing his horse in the muddy pool where she had quenched her thirst.

'What is this?' she asked.

'The sports page of the newspaper,' the man replied, concealing his surprise at her ignorance.

The answer astounded the girl, but she did not want to seem rude so she merely enquired about the significance of the fly tracks scattered across the page.

'Those are words, child. Here it says that Fulgencio Barba knocked out El Negro Tiznao in the third round.'

That was the day Belisa Crepuscolario found out that words make their way in the world without a master, and anyone with a little cleverness can appropriate them and do business with them. She made a quick assessment of her situation and concluded that aside from becoming a prostitute or working as a servant in the kitchens of the rich there were few occupations she was qualified for. It seemed to her that selling words would be an honourable alternative. From that moment on, she worked at that profession, and was never tempted by any other. At the beginning, she offered her merchandise unaware that words could be written outside of newspapers. When she learned otherwise, she calculated the infinite possibilities of her trade and with her savings paid a priest twenty pesos to teach her to read and write; with her three remaining coins she bought a dictionary. She pored over it from A to Z and then threw it into the sea, because it was not her intention to defraud her customers with packaged words. (Isabel Allende, *The Stories of Eva Luna*, 1991: 5–7)

Good and bad hits on the nose: 12th café

A: Do you believe that we can say that there is good talk and bad talk . . . like in this article of Penman's, you remember? Can the quality of talk be measured?

B: I guess so . . . why not?

A: You are just saying that to avoid going deeper into the topic.

B: Yes.

A: And you even admit that you say that to avoid going deeper into the topic?

B: Yes.

A: I will punch you on the nose!

B: Yes, please do.

    (*Both laugh*)

A: You are not interested?

B: Yes I am.

A: Is this good interaction we are having now?

B: I think so.

A: Why do you think so?

B: It feels quite good to me. You smile a lot too.

A: And why is it good?

B: Because we aren't saying anything which would turn it into a bad one.

A: And what would make it bad?

B: If you would really hit me on the nose, for example.

A: Why would it spoil the interaction?

B: Because I would prefer you not to do that.

A: You would not be participating in this joint process in a way you would want?

B: Exactly.

A: If you would like me to hit you on the nose it would be different?

B: Yes.

A: We would have good interaction then?

B: Yes.

A: So it is not hitting but participating in the planning of what happens next which matters?   *collaborative*

B: Yes, I think so.

A: Would you now like me to hit you on the nose?

B: No.

A: Still no? But isn't it good to ask? Things might change. I might not notice that at some moment you start to want to be hit on the nose. I would then treat you badly, in a way, not noticing and respecting what you want.

B: I could also develop an urge to hit you on the nose. Actually, I think it has already started to develop.

A: I get your message. But seriously, do you think that participation in deciding about the direction of where things go is the main thing in good interaction?

B: Yes, I think it is central. But it is still not the only thing. I think the metaphorical stuff is also important.

A: Tell me how you see it now.

B: I mean, in a more metaphorical context the directions are not so critical. The sense of direction is different. There is more freedom to define where we are and where we are going. The question of direction is not so important any more.

A: But people don't want to participate in metaphorical stuff if it does not feel promising or resonating or respectful for them. Participating in that kind of interaction requires a good atmosphere . . . quite a lot of security, an experience of not being wronged. So, these things are critical too.

B: So, we have three or four . . . or perhaps five critical things here . . . participation in decisions about direction . . . metaphori- cality . . . shared promise . . . maybe that comes close to resonance . . . experienced respect or safety.

A: I could sign that list.

Providential dialogues as solutions

What is common to the following situations: people sitting around a meeting table; lovers talking intensely with each other in a restaurant; a bunch of children playing football in the courtyard; counsellors and clients talking about what to do about the clients' difficulties?

In all of these situations people live in a shared world – they share a common framework of meaning. Knowing that 'communication' originally derived from the Latin 'commu- nicare', meaning 'to share', we could say that we have at our hands examples of 'communication', of sharing some- thing and behaving, thinking and feeling accordingly.

For us, communication is *not* transmitting information from one receiver/head to another but creating common episodes, commonplaces or shared temporary worlds (see Shotter, 1993a: 63–5). These, often rapidly changing, shared worlds are strange things. They each have their own (more or less vague) rules and their own temptations and despairs. Like games, they always support some possibilities, some forms of meaningfulness, some types of relationships and some moral orders – and not others.

We have learned from Bakhtin and social constructionists that these worlds are multi-layered, and complex. Like music or abstract paintings they have a huge *potential* for meaning: they always contain a multitude of specified, partly specified and yet-to-be-specified shapes. The experience of being in the same reality or the continuity of this reality can sometimes be shaken very easily (Garfinkel, 1967; Goffman, 1959).

The complexity of these temporarily shared worlds is, at least from a therapy perspective, a positive phenomenon – all kinds of issues, relationships and possibilities can be pointed to and drawn out because of it. This complexity also makes possible the sudden births and collapses of realities.

Robyn Penman, who has a strong interest in how different forms of linguistic interaction allow for participation, has written about 'good communication' from a post-modern perspective (Penman, 1992). Her views have a strong relevance to the main topics of this book. One of her conclusions is that 'goodness' has to be defined according to *moral* criteria. Good communication is what does good things to people: among its other possible tasks, it also expands people's possibilities and increases their experience of self-worth.

Penman uses four criteria to describe this kind of communication. First, communication has to start from the premiss that the talk (or text) in which we are participating constitutes the social realities of the moment (this criterion thus refers to the 'constitutiveness' of communication). Secondly, the communication has to be open to constant revision ('contextualness'). The third criterion is 'diversity'. A communication fulfilling this criterion recognizes the right of existence of other interpretations. The fourth criterion is 'incompleteness'. It means that neither communication, nor the meanings generated, can ever be complete or finalizable.

Translated into the terms we have been using, we could say that good communication leaves more of the interactive gaps visible; it respects the need for social connectedness

and also allows for the experience of moral worth by the
participants.

It seems to us that virtually everything in social life can be
conceptualized as a dialogue. This is obviously possible
regarding thinking, emotions and social interaction – and
regarding problems and solutions. It is both interesting and
useful to look at 'problems' discursively, through the metaphor of 'bad communication' (or interaction) in Penman's
sense. Using this starting point we could think of them, for
example, as 'difficult conversation partners', 'uninvited and
unwanted guests' or 'oppressors'. Common to all of these
perspectives is the predominance of monological and
awkward interaction forms. Problems are seen as representatives of truth-bearing, authoritarian, violent and foreign
voices.

If we start from the idea that people normally jointly
work to create contexts which allow them to go on and feel
promise and respect, we could think of problems as dis-
turbances in this process. We might also think that problems
are phenomena which make it impossible for the interaction
to fulfil Penman's criteria. If this seems a foreign and
abstract perspective, we might find it easiest to enter it by
considering personal experiences of awkward interactional
and communicational situations (monologues of authority
figures, excessively talkative colleagues, threatening behaviour, being denied participation, being bossed around and
so on).

Playfully about ludic: 13th café

A: I like these words . . . 'Dionysian ludism' . . . 'energetism' . . .
    'suspicion weighs on Prometheus' . . .

B: What is the book you are reading? What is ludism?

A: Ludism is playfulness, or it relates to play and playfulness . . .
    and this is a book by Maffesoli. I think we talked of him
    passingly some time ago. Remember?

B: 'The sociology of orgy'? (Maffesoli, 1993)

A: Yes. I think he is a professor of sociology at the Sorbonne . . . And the book is not about pornography or how to organize orgies, in case you might think that. It's about post-modernism, about the sacred, about pleasure, about sharing experiences . . . good stuff.

B: Let me see – that still sounds suspicious to me . . . knowing your mind . . . (*He leafs through the book for a while.*) I found a nice quotation. The chapter is 'Unproductive life': 'And since, in the ancient homeland of the Dionysian orgy and erotic knowledge, a puritanism of pedants reigns today, we need . . . a Rabelais or Restif de la Bretonne.' It is by Octavio Paz. And here is another. Maffesoli is saying that: 'productivism in its various forms has now become an object of criticism. Work and even progress are no more categorical imperatives . . . Suspicion weighs on Prometheus . . .' . . . You spoke about this before. I found the same place! It must be telepathy, a sign of . . .

A: No. You found it because the book was folded there. Give it to me. Thanks. It is my turn to read. Listen to this: 'one can say that the body, as a tool of production, is replaced by the erotic body'. I like this. There are nice chapter headings: 'Golden wine', 'Nigra sed pulchra' . . . it is about night, obscurity, darkness, 'Furious Eros' . . .

B: I think I'll have a glass of wine. For you, I recommend coffee . . . so you don't float any further in that direction. I take it he means erotic in a broad sense . . . looking at sensuality and sense enjoyment, to stand in contrast to the productivism of bodies just used to produce things . . . Could I ask you something? It is a rather stupid question . . .

A: You know I like stupid questions.

B: I mean . . . it is easy to think that there are different forms of language, different words, different rules for play and humour and for serious things. But are there? I mean, you can put a sentence to paper and it is not funny at all. Then you listen to somebody else say it and you can't stop laughing. Then yet another person says it, and it is serious again. The lightness is not in the words, it is somewhere else.

A: I agree. It is somewhere else. The difference between fun and serious can be minimal. I mean what is a sense of irony: a sense of having a slight distance between the words and what happens. I like the expression tongue-in-cheek. I mean, we often have to be serious and write seriously. It makes all the difference to have your tongue in your cheek.

B: But how do we know if somebody has their tongue-in-cheek . . . it might not be there?

A: I think you miss the point. It always is. We just don't always remember that it is. We cannot say things straight . . . it is an illusion.

B: But what does it then mean to have tongue-in-cheek?

A: You are starting to become obstinate. I think it is just a mood, a metaphorical orientation . . .

B: And the opposite of that is?

A: Knowing for certain and being really serious about it. You know the saying: 'a sergeant knows little but certainly'. Do you remember M's 'gigolo-analogy' of therapy. It sounded so outrageous. People asked him in the congress last year if he was serious about that.

B: I was not there. What did he say?

A: He smiled in a friendly way and said: 'Yes, it is serious' . . . and then, after a silence, '. . . but it is a little playful too'. That was a good answer, I think.

B: So, with problems people have difficulties with having a tongue-in-cheek attitude?

A: Yes, and it is possible to fall in two directions – to be too serious, or to be too light.

Contemplative moments

Contemplative moods

1   *To be with the one I love and to think of something else: this is how I have my best ideas, how I best invent what is necessary to my work. Likewise for the text: it produces, in me, the best pleasure if it manages to make itself heard indirectly; if, reading it, I am led to look up often, to listen to something else. I am not necessarily captivated by the text of pleasure; it can be an act that is slight, complex, tenuous, almost scatterbrained: a sudden*

movement of the head like a bird who understands nothing of what we hear, who hears what we do not understand. (Barthes, 1975: 24–5)

2   *Our habit has been to spend hours and hours in cafés on Saturdays and Sundays. We have our favourite places, but there has to be some variation too. We just sit and talk. There can be long silences. We try to find nice and interesting words and topics. These topics let you enjoy what you see in the café or outside. Thoughts and ideas fly smoothly like summer clouds. The skies are blue. Sometimes one of us starts to talk about practical matters and plans. That usually spoils the relaxed and enjoyable feeling . . . There is a sudden sense of constriction, a pressure to find right answers . . .*

3   *A clear autumn day, colourful leaves on the trees, the play of children, the home, classical music, music generally, children's songs, children's play, the moment of evening tea, the candles, the snow, the heaps of snow, skiing on the ice of the lake, a walk in the woods, rainy streets, the streets after the rain, the sea, the sail boats, the rocks, the sea landscape, rowing in the boat, the calmness of the sea, bouquets of flowers, guests at home, a party, the trees, good food, good drinks, nice conversations, the moments with my spouse, a movie accompanied by a glass of wine, summer dances, a wedding in a church, the church, the organ music, the silence, Christmas songs, spring creeks, first spring days, the dry spots of asphalt on the streets in spring, the scent of earth in spring, spring parties, Christmas parties at kindergarten, the presentations of children at them, walking hand in hand, parties with relatives, visiting friends, visits to grandparents, green plants, music in a green room, opera, theatre-evenings, a cosy restaurant, the autumn rain . . .*

(This was the first half of an answer to a home assignment on a 'Resource- and Solution-Oriented Client Work' course. The task was: 'Observe on three consecutive days, what is beautiful and/or inspiring for you'.)

Fixed gazes: 14th café

A: I have heard M say this many times, mostly in slightly different ways: 'When you have a problem, you have a fixed gaze.' It sounds very true to me. When people have problems they stare at something. Their eyes start to feel tired. There is no interest, no curiosity about details. They see only copies or recurrences of something. I think metaphors are the medicine for fixed gazes.

[margin note: problem = fixation]

B: We have talked of this but tell me again how you see it.

A: Metaphors give constant food for the mind . . . we find new things. If we start to believe in a model of mind or psychological problems, it is comparable to staring. In fact you could define science starting from that: 'science starts from curiosity and ends in staring'. From this perspective it is a bad thing to believe that you can do science with people.

B: I think movies are interesting in this respect. Some are so full of stares and stock phrases, some are so fresh.

A: I saw recently a movie where somebody obviously tried to ape Tarkovski. You know those slow water scenes in *Stalker* for instance . . . the camera follows water, moves over the water, looks through it for minutes. When I saw that scene for the first time I had the feeling that this is definitely somebody's perspective, definitely a momentary perspective of a definite person. In this other film there were water-scenes but it was like from a nature film. I just thought this is what brooks or small streams are . . . nothing personal whatsoever, nothing with a sense of life. And those cheap American TV series . . . there is nothing genuinely unexpected.

B: So what makes a difference?

A: I don't know. I think it has just to do with predictability. In bad movies or series the sentences and utterances really are dead. There is no tension between them. There are no pleasant or unpleasant surprises on their level. They are just filling material.

B: Juri Lotman said that the director of movies robs the audience of their eyes and gives them his or her own eyes. I think that when you have a stock phrase, something which really feels used, there is nothing of this. The audience can use their old eyes. There is no fight with the foreign viewpoint. In poetry there are several pairs of eyes. Each line or sentence can have a different worldview. They never fit totally. This not fitting is what helps to keep away from dead phrases.

A: I remember, in this Tarkovski water scene there were all kinds of objects seen under water: the camera moved slowly over them . . . they did not fit together at all . . . even if it was only one scene, there were many things happening . . . many interesting tensions.

B: But let's have another type of example. If somebody says to you: 'I hate this country, this way of life' . . . then, what do you say next? Something anti-cliché.

A: I think you could sometimes just start from the words them-selves. I listen quite a lot to the words. I can talk about a 'country' . . . 'What is your preferred country' . . . 'How is the country of your dreams?' . . . 'Do you like to be in the country?'. Or 'hate' . . . 'Does it turn in to other emotions sometimes?' Or I could talk about 'life' . . . 'love of life' . . . 'your love of life' . . . Julio Cortazar talked about somebody being under lives, over lives, between lives, inside lives, and so on. I could tell them about Cortazar and ask what they think they are inside or outside or between. But making these kinds of questions should be friendly. It should relate to their interests and desires. It should respect their suffering too. Often suffering is trivialized and made banal by giving advice – by stock phrases.

Inspiring topics

Choosing topics

The question which confronts us here is how to create providential contexts. What kinds of topics should be chosen? What kinds of interactional or dialogical forms have proved useful? The guidelines which can be outlined are necessarily rough and sketchy.

We all have abundant experience in everyday life of talk about interactional contexts which are dominated by problems and about the *relationship* that the participants have with problems – even if we are not always aware of speaking of these as relationships. Problem-dominated approaches are also still the mainstream in the world of therapy. However, it is as easy, and normally much more useful to focus on those interactional contexts when people have escaped from this dominance. This does not mean that it is always preferable to avoid problem-dominated stories and approaches, far from that. Many if not most people come to therapists and counsellors expecting to talk about their problems. Not letting them do that at any length or in any form could be disrespectful and create trouble.

It is thus to be expected that the initial topics are defined by the clients in terms of what is the problem. But even the initial complaints can be jointly negotiated. We can ask people: 'What is your problem?' or 'What goals do you think you would like to achieve?', or 'How might today's session be helpful for you?' All of these questions invite different types of topics in the conversation. If a couple are coming in because of their fights, there may be many different topics to choose from. For example: When do they talk well together? When do they listen to each other? Can they have an argument without it ending up being distressing? When have they experienced that they can agree to disagree? and so on. Choosing different topics will call forth different qualities of the persons and their rela-tionship – their warmth, their attentiveness, and so on.

We can at this point suggest some general, more or less interrelated criteria for preferred orientations to topics.

First, the topics have to be relevant (of interest) to the client. Many approaches clearly don't share this view – they are impositional and don't question their own practices of power.

Second, the topics should make *shared* interest possible. This means that they must fit somehow with the interests, ethical stances, theoretical frameworks and sense of justice of both therapists and clients. In clinical work, therapists probe and search around until they find topics of mutual interest.

The third criterion is promise: each topic will open possibilities for different actions and different meanings to be called upon; different types of discourse, different types of stories to be called forth. An important part of the process of seeking possible and promising topics is <u>sensitivity to small emotional shifts and movements</u>. People can suddenly appear more released or curious, for example. It is, of course, possible to ask directly about the interests or preferences of clients, but it is often the small movements and shifts of emotions and moral positions which give the most helpful clues about good directions for conversation.

The fourth criterion relates to dignity and justice. Different topics have different implications for the moral worth of the person – each of them has some implications.

These types of criteria can, of course, explain only a part of the actual choices of topics. Because of the reasons discussed previously, dialogues are by their nature quite jumpy and unpredictable. The choice of topics depends also on the constantly changing invitations of the situation created by the joint action of participants. Most of these invitations depend on factors which escape explanations. Not respecting them could create dialogical breeches.

Creating guidelines for the choice of topics is difficult also for other reasons. As we have claimed before, in connection with discussion about sacredness and good communication, there are also other types of needs which have to be respected. One of them relates to participation. Dialogical partners have to have a right to affect the flow of topics at all times. There are even more difficult demands: participants have needs related to undefinability and surprise. Without continuous injections of freshness and metaphoricality the inspiring powers of dialogue soon diminish.

Because of our close relationships to solution-focused brief therapy and narrative therapy it feels natural to comment about their contributions regarding providential contexts. We could say that the orientations of both approaches give some degree of safety as to the usefulness and promise of topics chosen when guidelines typical of them are followed.

→ participation - 50/50 balance in power over topic

For reasons relating to the 'goodness of communication' (Penman, 1992) described previously, however, following *any* principles will not guarantee a good result. The needs of keeping dialogues alive, safe and promising are more complicated than the rules any set of blueprints can offer.

What would it take to make tomorrow an 8 day? A client session

Therapist: *Hi!*
Client: *Hi!*
T: *Did you find a parking space?*
C: *Yes, thanks. It's quite difficult here nowadays.*
T: *Yes, it's getting really hard . . . So, what made you come in?*
C: *It's a long story.*
T: *We have time.*
C: *It's quite general. I am not happy with my life.*
T: *So how happy are you?*
C: *I said already, I am not very happy.*
T: *But I mean . . . let's say on a scale from 1 to 10. 'One' is not at all happy.*
C: *And 10?*
T: *As happy as you have ever been – even for short moments.*
C: *OK. Let's say 4 . . . 3 to 4.*
T: *Do you ever have better days?*
C: *Yes, sometimes, yes.*
T: *How high are you then?*
C: *Nowadays?*
T: *Yes.*
C: *Maybe at 7 to 8?*
T: *What's the difference . . . how do you know that you are at 7 or 8 . . . compared to 3 or 4?*
C: *I feel better. It is not so . . . I feel that I belong somewhere. I am not like a Martian.*
T: *Not like a Martian?*
C: *Yes. Now when I see people I think that I don't share anything with them. I feel like an outsider. I don't like the*

houses or landscapes or TV programmes. They are not for a person like me.

T: *So, how is it when you are at 7 or 8?*

C: *It's different. I kind of forget the things which feel bad when I feel bad. They don't disappear, they still exist, but I don't think of them so much.*

T: *So, what would it take to make tomorrow an 8 day?*

C: *It is not that predictable.*

T: *What's your best guess?*

C: *I could write something. I sometimes like writing. Something . . . which I feel promising. But it is not certain, I could end in feeling worse, if I get stuck.*

T: *What kind of writing?*

C: *Maybe short stories, bits and pieces of novels. I haven't published anything. Actually I have only started some pieces . . . I don't finish them.*

T: *So what is good in writing, when you don't feel stuck?*

C: *It is so . . . liberating. I mean the sky is not so low then, the walls are wider apart. I have a feeling that I still have imagination and some zest. I don't feel so drained any more.*

T: *When was the last time you wrote that?*

C: *A couple of days ago. But there have been long breaks before that.*

T: *How could you do more of that?*

C: *I don't know, that's a hard question. I am not a professional writer, you know.*

T: *So, what do you do?*

C: *I am a professor . . . of [. . .]. I am not very happy with that. People think it is a good thing to be a professor, but for me it isn't. It's mostly administration.*

T: *So would you rather be a writer?*

C: *Yes, yes I think so. But how to survive economically? There are no guarantees that I could make it.*

T: *What would make it more probable that you start writing . . . I mean seriously?*

C: *I don't know. Maybe encouragement. If a famous writer would say that I could do that. Or a couple of writers.*

Maybe if I could get something published and then . . . if the feedback was good.

T: *Something else?*

C: *I don't know . . .*

T: *Think of a miracle. Let's say there was a miracle tomorrow night . . . and after that you wouldn't need any more encouragement to start writing seriously. Then you would wake up and . . . How would you notice that there was this kind of a miracle?*

C: *A miracle . . . So you mean a real miracle?*

T: *As real as any miracle ever can be.*

C: [smiles] *That would be . . . I would just believe that I can really accomplish a good book. A feeling of strength. I don't feel too strong nowadays.*

T: *How would your colleagues in the university notice the change when you go there that morning?*

C: *They? Most of them wouldn't. Many are kind of . . . mummies, half-alive, half-human.*

T: *But some would? How?*

C: *Maybe . . . maybe I would be less avoidant. I avoid them because I don't have anything to say. I don't know, but I would maybe use more colourful language.*

T: *Some examples?*

C: *Just more personal . . . not so academic. I mean I might say something about my real sufferings and dreams.*

T: *So what would be the first step in that direction . . . when you decide to take the first step . . . what is it?*

C: *I will . . . I will . . . I could have a two–three week holiday, travel someplace . . . maybe to [. . .] . . . and take my laptop with me . . . I think that could be a way. I also know some people there. There would be some other reasons to go there too. In fact, I think that it could be a good idea.*
[The session continues.]

Relational knowing

John Shotter, in drawing on the work of Wittgenstein, suggests that instead of seeking what might be called

representational ≠ relation — associative
(is) (how)

representational understandings which seek to discover
what something *is*, that we may be concerned with relational understandings which suggest different possible ways
in which we might relate ourselves to our surroundings
(Shotter, 1993a, b). Wittgenstein writes that he is not concerned to 'hunt out new facts'. His work suggests a different
sense of understanding which relates to the practical nature
of our understanding. This means that we do not consider
understanding as 'taking in' new facts or in terms of
processes inside someone's head but consider it in practice,
that is 'in what sort of case, in what sort of circumstances,
do we say, "Now I know how to go on"' (Wittgenstein,
1953: § 154). That is to say, we can see understanding as
knowing how to go on, or more broadly, knowing how to
relate to our situation or circumstances. Thus understanding
indicates something about changed relationships and
knowledge is then about ways of relating to the world.
Knowing something gives us a way of relating, for example,
knowing that land has extractable minerals helps us mine it,
knowing that land is farmable helps us farm it, knowing
that land is sacred helps us revere and respect it and so on.

Most therapies, even those claiming to be social constructionist or post-modern, still use referential views of
understanding. In therapy, one way to understand what
we do is that we help people to have different relationships
to themselves, to their circumstances, their partners, their
lives.

This can take many forms. One form is what Michael
White calls externalizing the problem (White, 1989). If we
speak of the problem as a separate entity to the person, then
the person is free to relate differently to the problem.
Usually in externalizing the implied new relationship is
almost always one of fighting against the problem. The
metaphors are of the problem as a bully, tyrant, or trickster
and the client can then protest, escape, outsmart or over-
power the problem. For example, a child having difficulties
with soiling can put 'sneaky pooh' in its place (the toilet),
and become faster and stronger than sneaky pooh (White,

1989). Adults might 'stand up against' the influence of guilt in their lives. A couple might 'break free from' oppressive patterns of interaction.

In each of these examples we can see that defining or speaking of the problem as separate to the person allows new actions and possibilities. This implicitly occurs, we suggest, because a new relationship is present, so different types of knowledge and action become available. To put it in the terms we are exploring here, <u>the new relationship is a new knowledge</u>.

knowl.=
relationship

As well as fighting the problem, we might look at how it has been helpful or even a friend. Someone's anger which now seems uncontrollable may have in the past helped them to survive (e.g. Smith, 1988). Describing this may help them be more able to choose when to call on the anger or how best to express it. Someone's anxiety may be a warning sign that they are compromising their values or being caught in actions which may be against their better judgement if they reflected upon it. The anxiety may be a helpful voice.

There are many different types of new relational knowing, however. One which we have frequently alluded to in the book is the change of knowing/relating from seeing a situation as fixed and definite to seeing it as having possibility, alternative meanings, half-spoken associations.

Billig

In several articles and books the English social psychologist Michael Billig has emphasized the rhetorical and dilemmatic features of thinking (Billig, 1987, 1991). His view is that thinking is a form of arguing. It proceeds with the help of contrasting or oppositional concepts and discursive repertoires – with the help of the 'opposing horns of dilemmas'.

think=
argue

If we see thinking as dilemmatic, as a series of arguments and counter-arguments, we can also keep in sight the idea that any description really implies a relationship or a contrast with something else. The implied counter-arguments and counterpositions form a framework or pedestal which holds what is said together and makes it meaningful.

If clients' complaints are seen to consist of two-sided arguments, we can immediately become interested in their silent sides. If people give a description of themselves, what we hear is the dominant side of the argument, not the only possible one. It is indeed impossible to focus totally on restrictions and lack of possibilities. All expressions contain either direct or indirect signs of competence or hope (Riikonen, 1992; Riikonen and Mattila, 1994). Already, from the first words, we can hear the whisper of a whole range of other words in the background.

If someone describes himself or herself as 'weak', we can hear the contrast of 'weakness' with strength or sensibility or courage. We could ask questions like: When have they felt strong, clever or compassionate, or whatever for them might be the opposite of weakness? We can also ask questions like the following: Where did you get this idea that you are weak? How did that idea gain the ascendancy – how did that argument gain the high ground over other views? What ideas or experience have you had of not being weak? These all invite different relationships to the idea of weakness – of interest, curiosity or argument rather than being 'weighed down by' the description.

The type of description we co-create with our clients is crucial in this because it implies the type of relationship (understanding) to follow. If injustice is named, people can fight it rather than internalize it. Even if the surrounding systems do not change, the experience of the freedom fighter is very different from the experience of the slave or the 'depressive'. The experience of the person smiling at their human foibles is very different from the experience of the self-denigration of someone convinced they have failed to reach some specification for how to be a worthwhile person.

This type of relational knowing is something we are continually doing. We cannot not relate to our surroundings, nor to the topics of conversation. This goes on continually and is our knowing in action, our living of life, our knowing how to go on, or our feeling of stuckness and repetition.

Each of the metaphors presented in this book is a different way of knowing/relating. How we listen also suggests different ways of relating/knowing: listening to the description as a doorway to deeper meaning, or for 'the facts' for a diagnosis, or the horns of a moral dilemma.

From this perspective <u>knowledge is social and political. It is how we relate.</u>

Providential listening

The response creates the meaning: 15th café

A: I'll write a couple of sentences on the paper (*silence*) . . . like this. The x's are whatever words:

> xxxxxx xxx xxxxx xxxxx . . . Our life is horrible . . . xxxx xxxx xxxxxxxx xxx xxxxxx xxxxx . . . I like children . . . xxxxx xx xxxxx . . . I felt closer . . . xxxx xxxx xxxx xxxxx . . . It was a nice period . . . xxxx xxxxx xxxx xxxx . . . during that trip I felt OK . . . xxx xxxxxx . . . I like horror movies . . . xxxx xxx

B: So what is that?

A: Wait for a moment . . . This first visible real sentence here . . . I underline it . . . so . . . is the client's problem description . . . '<u>Our life is horrible</u>'. There is talk after and before it . . . all the x's. As a response to this sentence . . . what could we say . . . I mean . . . if it is <u>the response which creates the meaning</u> of what was said?

B: We could say something like . . . 'What makes you think so?' . . . 'It will end, you have made it before' . . . 'What exceptions are there?', 'The sun will shine after the rain' . . . or something else.

A: In a way these are all quite traditional responses. What kind of meanings do they make? At least they create factuality regarding 'the horrible life'. They start from the premiss that life really *was* horrible. On the other hand the last two comments prepare ground for the idea that the horrors might end.

B: You always say that my responses are traditional.

A: You are a classic . . . that's the reason.

B: Thanks.

complaining— complaint – desire
choice

A: And . . . and then there are these other sentences after that. What is their relationship to the first? We could connect them to the complaints in many different ways. We could say that the first group of questions you asked react to the hopelessness of the sentence . . . or that they kind of respect it. They make these sentences into social facts. But on the other hand we know that complaints also imply frustrated wishes. There are two sides to all complaints . . . the complaining side and the desire side . . . and we can react to either of them.

B: So what? And this is a friendly 'so what'.

A: Yes, I see that. I mean . . . combining something containing something nice to the complaint makes the complaint kind of suspect in a nice, quiet way. Doing this creates fissures to the hopelessness, in a way. But how to do that in this case? That's the question. There could be straight questions like: 'How does it affect your view of the situation that you like children . . . or . . . that you had such a nice time?' Or: 'Does it make it easier or more difficult to go on when you know that you had those good times?' But there could be other ways too. These kinds of things make the complaint sound as . . . I can't find a word . . . not a 'fact', but only 'a couple of words'. Like you can sometimes say 'you bastard' in a way which feels friendly. Turning facts to mere words or figures of speech. I think we come back to the tongue-in-cheek problematic here.

B: Let's try . . . 'you f—ing bastard'!

A: See . . . I don't hit you . . . I am quite calm (*suddenly tries jokingly to hit B*) . . . But I changed my mind . . . I think you meant it as a fact after all. Words are dangerous, you see.

Listening as a transformative process

Traditional understandings of listening in therapy have tended to be informed by views of language which we have critiqued throughout the book. According to the traditional understanding, the therapist 'takes in' the facts of the situation. Listening itself is not seen as an active or influential process. However, a dialogical view suggests the very nature of the person with whom we speak is partly constructed through the manner of our listening.

In most forms of therapy (with notable exceptions like psychoanalysis), especially in fields of cognitive therapies and family therapies, the emphasis has been on intervention or questioning. Listening has been taken for granted. This neglect means there is often little differentiation between different types and styles of listening.

A dialogical perspective to listening underlines its active nature. Bakhtin describes dialogue as always having both 'addressivity' and 'receptivity'. We can never speak out of a vacuum nor into one. In addressing someone we will be conscious of whom we are addressing and how they might respond. Our expectations concerning the other person's responsiveness will affect our manner of presentation, the details selected, the values appealed to, and so on. Even in thinking to ourselves, the manner of our self talk (the genre, the emotions appealed to, the experiences accessed, the roles adopted etc.) will be influenced or determined by the 'audience' to which we speak. In therapy, we provide this receiving context for our clients. We have types of receptivity that influence what is said and how it is said.

As examples of different types of listening one could consider the manner used by cross-examining barristers (in which they look for inconsistencies in what the examinees are saying, weaknesses in their arguments, ways of making them appear corrupt or stupid or confused), by a traditional academic hearing a presentation (actually much like the barrister, looking for inconsistencies, weaknesses in the argument, issues not addressed etc.), by a friend having fun at a party (listening for double meanings of words or ambiguities from which to make jokes), by a doctor making a differential diagnosis (listening for only very specific 'facts', such as headaches and sleep disturbance) and so on. If we had to talk to the barrister in court or the friend at a party our presentation and sense of self would be quite different. Similarly, if we give a professional presentation to a group of colleagues or are playing with a child, not only what we say but who we feel ourselves to be will be quite different. In therapy if we listen for pathology, facts, or the mystery of a person we will not only find different information, but our manner of receptivity will influence who it is that we are interacting with.

Neglecting this means there is little differentiation between different types of listening and this is significant as style of listening is one of the most important factors in determining the type of session one has, what 'information' is presented and the type of person with whom we experience working.

Let us consider some different practical aspects of listening. First, there is the question of whether or not the client feels understood. Research into clients' experience of therapy consistently finds that 'being understood' is one of the most important things for clients in deciding whether or how therapy has been helpful. In the light of the other issues discussed in this book we can now re-approach this idea of understanding in a new light. To start with, it should be clear that understanding is not simply a question of 'taking in the facts' – feeling understood is very much a question of moral knowing, specifically that we can hear what the person is saying from the perspective of believing that they are a morally worthwhile person. This most usually means that we can see the events they describe in the context of a narrative which is exemplary of some values they and we support (or prize). These narratives usually then allow the explanation of 'bad' behaviour or feelings in terms which allow a moral regrading. Specific ways of achieving this include identifying restraints which prevented them from acting or thinking in a different way at the time; or seeing the problem in terms of its inevitability; or seeing it as the result of external injustice; or recognizing a sacrifice which had been hidden. A less frequent but not uncommon alternative is to have a narrative of a turning point where someone changes from an old to new way of being and acting – this usually hinges around a change of emotional stance (for example, expressions of remorse) or in different

being undastood
 – knowledge – how well can you relate

contexts it may link with 'salvation' or acceptance of limitation (for example, A.A. type models). In these situations the
old ways are seen as wrong but the person is seen to have
separated from these old ways.

Secondly, listening links with issues of power. The stance
of 'not knowing' (cf. Anderson and Goolishian, 1988) is a
manner of listening which can invite a mutual exploration of
experience, whereas the traditional expert role means the
determination of what is significant remains entirely with
the expert. In this latter instance the client may accept that
'doctor knows best' but is not likely to feel understood in
anything but the most limited way.

Therapy can also be seen as a ceremony of degradation or
regradation (Epston, 1989). Listening and responding in a
way which classifies the client as 'other' is implicitly
degrading them because it assumes the right to comment on
them as knowable and implicitly categorizable. This is a
defining and limiting act, and as Bakhtin has said,
unfinalizability is a crucial part of being human.

Thirdly, the concepts we have of the person will influence
our manner of listening. A discursive understanding suggests that people become constructed in particular ways
because of discourses within which they have lived. That is,
each person has had a unique position in terms of particular
sets of discourses within which they have developed –
discourses from their family of origin, their peers, and cultural and subcultural discourses concerning how to be moral
or valued, how to make sense of the world and so on. From
this perspective we cannot fully know someone else but can
begin to explore their histories of discourse. And we cannot
take the expert role to know more than they do; only to have
different knowledge and skills in conversation.

Fourthly, listening is not a passive procedure. Most people
will not feel understood if the person to whom they are
speaking sits there and does not respond and this response is
usually what the listener says. Part of this can be simple
words of agreement or paraverbal responses like 'uh-huh',
but these in themselves do not convey understanding. The

listener will usually from time to time make some statements or questions to 'feed back' their understanding or to seek clarification ('Was it more like this or this?'). In doing this the listener is offering alternative descriptions to the other person, and each alternative description will imply different ways of relating to their experience, different possible stances, and different ways of shaping their experience. At this point we are in the <u>process of shaping meaning</u> which is arguably the most important aspect of therapy. We are also offering choices of description to the client so that they can choose a type of description which 'feels right' for them – this may often include choices which they had not considered or were unable to articulate. These choices may imply quite different discourses, such as exploring how someone had suffered oppression as opposed to how they had personal inadequacies.

Offering different emotion words is also highly significant here as each of these implies different orientations, evaluations and possibilities for future action and motivation. Part of what we are doing in the early stages of therapy is helping people find words or expressions of their experience which feel comfortable and accurate for them. For example, someone might say that they have been 'really down' about the way someone has been treating them, and we might ask, 'when you say "down" do you feel more sort of depressed or hurt or angry or despairing . . ..' Sometimes of course the reply may be 'just down', but often the articulation of the feeling in terms which imply different distinctions feels more accurate and introduces different possibilities for responding (even when someone does say 'just down' they often add 'I just can't explain it any other way', as if searching for an alternative). If there is a different description, which feels preferable (more accurate, more moving, more resonant), different possibilities immediately open. Any different description implies having a different way of relating and is often what enables a person to say 'now I can go on' – to understand in the Wittgensteinian sense. For example, instead of just 'feeling down', if the person describes their despair, or their frustration, or the injustice they have suffered, each of these implies different ways to go on (for example, to regain hope, to explore the impediments to their goals, how to protest or escape from that injustice).

Finally, we also have our own emotional response. We can respond with warmth, concern, indignation or 'cold detachment', and each of these in turn implies an evaluative position, which will influence the person with whom we speak.

Café or not? 16th café

A: By the way, have you noticed that as the book goes on it seems to have become more and more cafés and less and less 'real' academic writing?

B: Yes, I had. Anyway, where are we now – in a coffee shop or in the book somehow, as some sort of abstracted self-reflexive figures?

A: I'm not sure I can tell any more.

B: I hope it's a café. I could use a cappuccino.

Finding providential metaphors

Le misfit[1]

When the clock asks for the right time
I'll answer
When the map asks for the right road
I can be the guide
To the compass I will show all of the directions
But to these questionnaires I
can never fit

J. Leskinen, 'Mo'om' in *Äeti*,[2] 1994: 33

---

[1] In the Finnish version, an English article is used, 'The Sopeutumaton'.

[2] The word 'mother' (*äiti*), pronounced in the Savo style. Savo is one of the eastern districts of Finland.

Diagnosis as a cure

A group of managers were asked to describe some social, psychological or cooperational problems in their respective companies which they would like to be resolved. After this they were encouraged to think of a new diagnosis for these problems. The diagnosis had to fulfil several criteria: it had to be credible, it had to 'save faces' (as many as possible), and it had to feel useful/promising in the sense that it could inspire effective future action. It soon became apparent that in many cases this change of situational definitions and labels was all that was needed to untie the described knots.

An almost hopeless couple

Client: *I don't think we have much hope as a couple any more. We quarrel all the time nowadays. In fact I am starting to think that I am quite hopeless myself. I don't get along . . .. Remember, I was seeing you before with my previous partner. We quarrelled all the time too.*

Counsellor: *When do you have your best moments in your relationship now?*

Client: *We have good moments . . . but really . . . only when we prepare food and make love . . . [long silence] . . . maybe when we walk on the beach . . . [laughs]. Thinking more about it, we might still have hope . . .*

Bad left foot

A father of a pre-adolescent boy who is a very good football player explained that the boy was recently quite depressed after making a series of severe mistakes in a certain game. The father (who is also coach of a boy's football team) told the boy that he thinks that most of the mistakes depend on the problems with his left foot. Many times the left foot spoils it all, even if the boy himself does everything quite OK. The father told the boy to give a real lesson to the left foot and to have it under special surveillance from now on.

Providential diagnostics

It has become apparent in many chapters that from the perspective of theory the process of jointly creating providential contexts is a very complex task. Yet it can progress with an amazing ease and incredible speed in many settings. In contrast to this, joint negotiations about meanings of psychiatric diagnostic labels and definitions can be quite time-consuming. It is often very hard for the clients to detach themselves from the implications and prescriptions they see contained in the labels.

Naming is a very powerful act (see especially Tamasese and Waldegrave, 1993). Once we name something, we distinguish it. The naming of mental, invisible and experiential phenomena helps to distinguish them. This allows us to take a position in relation to them in our conversations and actions. To make decisions, to be an agent, presupposes a distance between the actor and the thing acted upon. Naming can be seen as a special instance of forming such distances. Increased distance and visibility have immediate implications for oppressed groups. Naming social injustice often marks the beginnings of a person separating from the effects of that injustice, at least as it affects their sense of self. Even if the injustice continues, it becomes easier for the person to identify their strengths and stories in the face of it.

It is often useful to talk with people about what name they might want to give to their difficulties. The names can be idiosyncratic to the person. As such they are more powerful and useful than the 'packaged words' of psychological texts. Clients have in our experience called their difficulties names like the 'maze', 'the black cloak', 'the cloak of invisibility' or 'the rejection plague'. They have talked of how to 'find their direction', 'throw off the cloak', or 'avoid the old responses like the plague'. Giving a name made it easier to discriminate what relationship they wanted to have to old patterns and new possibilities.

We should not be talking only about problems. Also naming hopes, developments or goals is often very useful. Interestingly, there is often a sense of depth and sacredness to the forming of descriptions of problems and hopes because the process gives shape to the 'not-yet-said', half-felt, and as yet unformed areas of the person's experience. This process does in a very real sense shape and form the person.

DSM-type diagnoses are a good example of foreign words in dialogues. From the perspective outlined above, objectivistic diagnostic systems are problematic from the beginning, because they represent the voice of the absolute authority of science. Often, however, the clients succeed in utilizing the labels to their own benefit by creating their own meanings for them. Sometimes the joint process of detoxifying the diagnosis is one of the main tasks in therapy/counselling sessions.

One of the authors (G.S.) recently saw a woman client who thought she had a 'depressive personality', because her doctor had said that to her. Having described herself as a depressive personality there seemed to be nothing that was worthwhile for her to do any more. She initially thought that she could never overcome this obstacle. To her the words of this diagnostic formulation were totally foreign words. She could not question or make them ironic in any way. They were an absolute prescription for her. However, as she started exploring different elements of her experience and the meanings the words of the diagnosis might imply, she left this view behind.

In a contrasting case a female client of the other author (E.R.) had been told that she suffered from 'unspecified personality disorder'. In the first therapy session she wanted to know if having that diagnosis was good or bad news. Before she had time to get an answer, she said that she felt it was good news. Now she had to do all kinds of things which were good for her to cure herself from this disorder. Who could have created a better strategy?

Using moral imagination

> *It follows that, like every other general psychological theory, it*
> *[the form of psychotherapy] must be assessed, not for*
> *verisimilitude, but in relation to some moral order, that is,*
> *with respect to the kinds of lives belief in it enables people to*
> *live. (Harré, 1983: 284)*

> *What personal development is possible will depend on the*
> *theories actors hold. Certain person-theories will promote self-*
> *knowledge and mastery, others will inhibit them. (Harré, 1983:*
> *256)*

Moral-imaginative disorder: 17th café

A: I would still like to talk about how to find words . . . topics . . .
     metaphors . . . which help to bring about shared promise and
     which resonate for all. We should talk more about the moral
     dimension of that.

B: I agree.

A: It is such a complex goal. I mean, so many conditions have to
     be met at the same time. I am speaking now only of therapy.
     Part of the task is to help people to find words . . . which can
     help them to describe their experience in a way which
     resonates for them. Instead of taking on an expert's description
     of themselves, it could be more useful to find descriptions that
     feel meaningful . . . or rich . . . or accurate for them. I think
     these things are often outside dominant or habitual discourses.

B: What you say re-so-nates with my experience of working with
     people.

A: Good for you.

B: I mean, those official descriptions often don't help people to
     do anything new or feel better. So, if someone has been
     described as weak . . . These kinds of negative labels often
     seem to describe everything for the person. But let's say . . . she
     could also sincerely see herself as 'principled' or 'caring' or as
     'concerned'. Each of those words and metaphors could fit her
     experience. Underlining them could really open up different
     ways of seeing herself. So, we can work with words and

metaphors somewhat tentatively, to try to find descriptions that are different and yet true for the people. I think this is particularly important when people have suffered injustice. They can often find a way to describe their experience in ways that don't mean just taking on the dominant discourse.

A: Do you have any good examples of that?

B: One example of that is marginalized groups. Habitual descriptions of marginalized groups' experiences are often formulated using a psychiatric discourse. These people are seen as depressive or antisocial . . . or whatever else it might be. There is often very little attempt to understand that the way of life or experience can have something to do with living in a marginalized culture. One survey I read which was looking at difficulties experienced by African Americans, found that 80 per cent of descriptions of the problems they had were put in internalized individual terms. The perspective is normally individualistic . . . there is something wrong with the individual as an individual . . . they are too this or they are too that.

A: So?

B: So . . . These approaches deny social realities . . . injustice, poverty, discrimination, oppression. And these experiences must be respected, and the injustices named for what they are. To just give a label to a person denies all that. If we cannot respect people's experience, we cannot create and maintain shared topics which are promising for all participants.

A: Do you think that this condition would deserve a diagnosis 'Lack of social and moral imagination'? I think that to have a diagnosis like that in DSM-IV would be useful in many ways. I am only joking.

B: It is not a joke really. I mean it would make much more sense to have a diagnosis like that than most of the existing ones.

Views to morality

Moral threat seems to effectively rigidify methods people use for solving social or psychological problems. But what is moral? And what is the relationship of moral threat and imagination? What is the role of moral questions in therapy?

It feels necessary to give some thought to general issues regarding morality before embarking on discussion of the relationship between morality and therapy. If this is not done, we can easily stick to rather outdated ways of thinking of moral matters and problems.

Morality can be defined more widely as consisting of reasoning about what is valuable or good and what lacks worth or is bad. According to this view moral reasoning consists of attempts to find 'the right thing to do'. When morality is described in this way, it is obvious that moral issues are very relevant to human problems. Neither psychological problems nor their solutions can be understood without reference to what is felt to be good, natural, obligatory or serious. A person visiting alien cultures always has difficulties in understanding the psychological sufferings, conflicts and pressures of the locals. So, it seems clear that at least a part of the process of solving problems has to be a moral venture. Because of this, it is useful to look at some recent theories of moral deliberation.

Charles Taylor has emphasized that morality is usually understood too narrowly (1989). He claims that the concept of the 'moral' can be thought to include at least three dimensions: it can be seen as referring (i) to fulfilling norms and obligations regarding right conduct, (ii) to leading a full and meaningful life and (iii) to dignity. Taylor's ideas are interesting especially because he argues that identities and moral issues relate to each other tightly and that moral deliberation is to a great extent narrative and imaginative. According to him people create their identities in the context of, and as responses to, the demands of situationally and historically changing images of right and wrong, good and bad.

Also cognitive science is relevant in this context. Recent studies in cognitive sciences imply that both our concepts and our reasoning are structured by various kinds of imaginative processes (Johnson, 1993: 1). Since moral reasoning makes use of the same cognitive capacities it is also imaginative by its nature.

Of course, there is a long history of debate about understandings of morality. Our interest is in the predominant view which seems to inform both psychology and the day-to-day thinking of Western culture at large. This view considers morality basically as rule-following. Moral reasoning is seen as discerning the appropriate moral rules which tell us what to do in a given situation.

Moral objectivism and the objectivistic 'moral law folk theories' form the theoretical basis for models of everyday moral reasoning. These kinds of models presuppose that we possess a universal, disembodied reason that generates absolute rules, decision-making procedures and universal laws by which we can tell right from wrong in any situation. Mark Johnson's view of morality is in strong contrast with this view. He claims that moral reasoning is a constructive imaginative activity which is based principally on metaphoric concepts in two different ways: first, fundamental moral concepts like will, freedom, law, right, duty and so on, can only be defined metaphorically; secondly, the way we conceptualize situations in which moral questions are relevant depends on the use of metaphors making up the common understanding of members of our culture.

There are different ways to undermine the role of imagination in moral reasoning. Moral absolutism asserts the existence of universally binding, absolute moral laws that can tell which acts, experiences and desires are right and which are wrong. It assumes that 'imagination' is merely subjective and that it has no place in moral reasoning. The opposite position, moral relativism, argues either that there are no moral laws of any sort, or that if there are, they could have force only relative to a particular cultural group, and within a particular historical context. If moral relativists talk about imagination, they do so because they regard it as unconstrained, as opposed to reason, and as undermining the idea of moral universals (Johnson, 1993: 3).

The idea contained in both moral absolutism and relativism, that imagination is non-rational is, of course, deeply problematic. This way of thinking has its roots in faculty psychology which assumed totally distinct and functionally independent capacities of the mind's different faculties. According to this logic, reason was regarded as the calculative part of self, the purpose of which is to see true descriptions and to formulate principles. This machine of the mind wants nothing itself. Desire, the moving and active part of the self, was seen as the faculty by which the self determines the objects of its appetites and aversions. It motivates us and moves us towards objects and states of being that can satisfy our interests and wants. Desire, unaided by understanding, can see or understand nothing.

There have been two responses to this problem of bifurcation in Enlightenment moral theory; emotivism and the Kantian rationalist strategy. The response of emotivism was that reason and desire cannot be brought together, and that morality is only a matter of desire or feeling, located entirely within the non-rational realm of being. Kant's strategy was to claim that reason must somehow be united with desire to produce a reason which is truly practical. There is, however, no way of proving that reason really can be practical in this sense. Kant tried to show that there is no solution to the problem unless its terms are redefined.

The only working solution seems to be to undo the split. This is actually attempted by cognitive sciences, which see humans as fundamentally imaginative creatures. Metaphors and imaginative structures give us alternative viewpoints and concepts which can be used to evaluate the pros and cons of particular moral positions. They also make it possible to envision the probable and possible consequences of a planned course of action. Imagination can thus give us answers regarding how people are likely to be affected, how the action might change relationships, and what new possibilities might open up or close off.

What makes disconnected events into sequences of meaningful and moral actions is the synthetic unity supplied by cognitive models, metaphors, frames and narratives. Narrative is often seen as the most comprehensive form of synthetic understanding. Moral reasoning and moral imagination should therefore be examined in a narrative context.

Many representatives of psychology and family therapy argue that humans are unavoidably story-producing creatures; almost everything touched by humans turns into a narrative. Jerome Bruner has maintained that people simply do not have any other means of making their lives and experiences understandable, and preferably also making them examples of virtues of some type or another (Bruner, 1986, 1987).

Living a life with some notion of human flourishing is indeed one of our chief problems: 'We each want very badly for our particular life stories to be exciting, meaningful and exemplary of the values we prize' (Johnson, 1993: 180). Morality is thus in large part a matter of how well we construct and live out a narrative that solves our continuous problem of living a meaningful and worthwhile life.

The process of our everyday narration and moral brico- lage is greatly helped by the abundance of resources for moral imagination. Philosopher Alistair MacIntyre has con- centrated on the fragmentariness of our moral conceptions and moral reasoning (MacIntyre, 1981). He has claimed that talk and thinking about the moral lies above emptiness. We talk about moral issues, connecting with other concepts, which at some period of time have had significance but which now have been disjointed from their original contexts and meanings – and nobody seems to notice this.

There are many ways in which the view of morality as thoroughly imaginative can benefit the practices of helping. One of the important assets of this view is that it can be used to connect many different traditions and practices of therapy; they can all be seen as methods which enhance processes of moral imagination.[3]

---

[3] What has been said so far does not mean that psychological help has to deal openly with moral issues to be successful. We can, for example, have a 'purely behavioural' therapeutic approach and yet work with moral issues on a grand scale – unknowingly, and possibly even denying this.

What is still clearly needed are attempts to describe the connections of moral imagination and relational perspectives in more detail. In the next chapters we will try to move in this direction and make efforts towards linking moral questions and moral imagination to some of the central topics of helping – trust, validation and emotional experiences.

De-colonization, re-connection

It would be strange to talk about help and psychotherapy and bypass the themes of trust and validation. The trouble is that these topics are hard to approach from a discursive perspective. It is easy to slip into a way of talking which could be described as 'moral high ground'. This orientation can produce seemingly endless lists of nice words and well-meaning principles. A more interesting attempt is to try to understand something about how phenomena like trust and validation really can be produced in dialogues. Many relevant themes and concepts have been already discussed but there are still some points which merit a more thorough examination.

The concept of 'accountability' refers to discursive mechanisms by which people maintain trust and respect in relationships. These mechanisms prevent and repair social breaches and psychological hurts. Their workings presuppose shared moral frameworks. Without a common moral framework we would lack a basis for repair work. One of the basic preconditions of accountability is a willingness/ capability to take each other's hurts seriously – a breakdown of accountability means that there is a lack of interest in regard to hurt and suffering.

One important feature of breaches of accountability is that oppressors and/or targets of oppression are not necessarily conscious of the situation. 'Colonization' is one metaphor for this state of affairs. For the process to be successful the colonized have to believe that the colonizer has a greater moral worth than they. In 'ideal' cases the colonized try to become like the colonizer.

In an analogous way, we can think of persons experiencing psychological difficulties as accepting someone else's negative description of them as a truth. This is indeed clearly the case with many victims of psychological or physical violence. An abused person easily may tend to see him/herself as not really worthwhile, or as worthy of only being abused. It is also quite common for people to blame solely themselves for their misfortunes, even if they belong to an obviously oppressed racial or minority group.

A part of the process of de-colonization consists of redefining one's relationship to oppressive social and cultural practices. The process of distancing oneself from these practices can be started with questions like the following:

- Where do you think these oppressive descriptions come from?
- Which other types of descriptions/voices in you have been silenced?
- Have you thought differently to these voices?
- Have you been able to listen to other ideas?
- What might it mean if you were able to listen more to those different ideas?
- How might you find a different balance of voices?

To use words like 'colonization' is, of course, in many ways problematic. One of the difficulties is that the word seems to imply a unitary oppressor or a unitary oppressed self. What we should be talking about is not so much the self but the construction/destruction of possibilities and resources in speech. We should perhaps refer to systems of accountability as ways of speaking which help the person who feels wronged to be heard by others, especially by the person whom they perceive to be the wrong-doer.

There have been interesting developments around the theme of accountability at The Family Centre at Lower Hutt in New Zealand, and following their lead also at Dulwich

Centre in Adelaide (Hall, 1994; Tamasese and Waldegrave, 1993; Waldegrave, 1990). One of the key ideas has been to let one group speak while another group functions as a 'listening group'. Many of the conversations revolve around particular issues, for example, gender-related experiences. The conversations proceed in cycles during which each group describes their experiences and views regarding particular events while the other listens. This method seems to make it possible both to be supportive and to be able to speak freely of difficult issues. It also seems to generate respect and possibilities to repair the breaches.

The feeling of being heard is extremely important for most people. A matrix of trust means knowing that the other person will make a genuine attempt to hear, and to acknowledge the experience of being wronged.[4] It also means trusting that the experienced wrong-doer at least to some degree understands the descriptions of what has happened. We could also say that one aspect of account-ability has to do with making some hurts visible. The visibility is important because people often experience hurt exactly at those times when they feel that their experience has been made invisible or insignificant. It is, however, not only experiences of hurt, but also ideas about mutual moral positions which should be rendered visible – people often have all kinds of misleading ideas about them.

But how can we define these positions? It would be tempting to think that only one moral order prevails at one moment of interaction but this could be wishful thinking. MacIntyre's claim is probably appropriate: everyday life is a quite chaotic ensemble of different moral orders, compar-able to different games with different rules (MacIntyre, 1981). A big part of social interaction seems to relate exactly to defining and redefining these orders. Indeed, interper-sonal difficulties may not relate so much to the experiences

---

[4] Expressions like 'moral matrix' may be misleading. It might be better to speak of people moving between different moral orders. We don't say that different games – football, ice hockey, billiards, chess, solitaire etc. – form a 'big game'.

of hurt in themselves but to the assumptions about the moral positions.

One of the complications of defining positions is that usually when people are in a position of more power, often the type of power they have is less visible to them (it is only lack of felt resistance and this feels quite natural). People *power* who are in positions of lesser power can more easily see the workings of power. For these reasons it is important to see moral positions, accountability and visibility of hurt as forming a whole.

Functional ways of hearing and responding to the hurts form a basic mechanism for helping and for maintaining good relationships with others. But there are also other important factors which need to be touched upon in this connection. A related need is making a person's good qualities and intentions visible. This process can be described using the word 'validation'.

Our descripton of validation is that it involves making a person's (or group's) actions, qualities, experiences and positions understandable and acceptable. The concept refers not only to acknowledging explicit goals, emotions or motivations, but also to possible and more acceptable (or more noble) ones. Validation thus obviously has to do with treating people well.

E-motion

E-moving together: 18th café

A: I will go back to one of the old themes. Perhaps the simplest way to understand therapy is to start from a lack of motion or fluidity. And then emotions are a central thing. They are about motion.

B: I agree.

A: So this is the basically Wittgensteinian point: problems are difficulties of being locked into a place or position – not knowing how to go on. I think that being able to go on is mostly connected to moral issues. People want to find ways to go on *and* maintain a face. You know Ben and Tappi,[5] who see therapy as 'moral aerobics' or even as 'moral acrobatics'. They think that the goal is to find ways of speaking and thinking of problems and solutions which are morally acceptable to all involved. I think that this way of looking at things has an instant appeal.

B: So, the message is that when there is a moral problem – somebody is too hurt or something – people get stuck. The ideas get stuck and the emotions get stuck.

A: Yes . . . but.

B: With you it's always yes but . . . yes but, yes but, yes but.

A: Whenever you get irritated by an innocent yes–but, I know that your blood sugar is running low. We have to order something more. I mean that the movement thing is quite complex. There are many things involved. I have tried to find something to read about this but no. I am so pissed off with these books on linguistics and linguistic philosophy. It is such a jumble. There is nothing about movement. I mean speech is moving . . . I don't mean only emotions . . . when we speak we are moved from one thing to another . . . from one role to another . . . from one situation to another . . . from good to bad, and so on.

B: I agree. But it all stems from the old fact that words and talk are usually seen not as action, but as messages. I was looking at these pantomime actors at the fringe-festival . . . you remember? If you look at them it is so clear that gestures and signs are all action. But in speech and especially in written texts, it is easy to forget that what we produce are actions. To return to this Bakhtin-stuff . . . 'the utterance, not the word or sentence, is the basis of communication'. It is so much clearer. The utterance is part of interaction.

A: I agree this movement stuff is important because the concept of emotion we have had is so strange – emotion described as just something people have . . . like measles. It is partly about

[5] Ben Furman and Tapani Ahola, Finnish brief therapists.

moving others and ourselves to positions and roles. So, I think it is a good idea to underline the motion stuff. It also helps in not glossing over the moral dimension . . .

B: I like what you just said. It makes many things more visible.

Emotion and therapy[6]

One of the noteworthy features of emotions is that they are ambiguous. This is true even with strong, and at first sight distinct emotions: if someone feels angry we may find that the anger is linked with a feeling of hurt – or frustration – or powerlessness. Correspondingly, if someone feels intimate it may be linked with feelings of acceptance – or approval – or joy – or with something else.

To feel implies to orientate oneself, to have a stance, to take a position. Emotion words and emotion talk are particularly important in shaping and forming relationships and social interaction. Emotions can be seen as a complex constellation of feelings, volitions, motivations, organizing principles in relationships and also as comments on role status. This way of understanding emotion talk seems much richer than just seeing emotion talk as labelling feelings. From this viewpoint emotion talk has particular implications for the definition of the characters of the people with whom we speak.

To understand someone's emotions and feelings is to understand their position within interactions. Interestingly, seeing emotions as relational stances and positionings also sheds new light on 'rationality' and 'emotional coldness'. From this perspective, a person adopting a position which is 'coldly rational', is just adopting a different type of emotional position – rather than having an absence of

[6] We wish to acknowledge particularly the backdrop of many discussions and interactions of Gregory Smith with Jane Tiggeman in providing a context for fresh understandings of emotion and the practical knowledge of this in day-to-day interactions.

emotion. The 'coldly rational' position can usually be seen
as disaffiliative and as an attempt to gain superiority in one
sense or another. One correlate of emotional coldness is that
power the person is usually claiming privileged access to certain
knowledge.

Many of our everyday terms for describing emotion
reflect a traditional metaphor of emotions being objects in a
container, that is, the person. For example, we speak of how
people 'display emotion', 'express emotion' or 'allow their
emotions to show', all of which assume that emotion is
something within the person which people can then allow to
'come out'. Emotions have also been seen as being in
marked distinction to rationality, and devalued in relation
to it.

All this is consistent with a general 'mind–body' split
which has been commonplace in Western thought. Emotion
is usually linked with the body, the body usually being the
devalued half of this 'mind–body' split. This split has a long
history and is often referred to as a Cartesian dualism,
following the eighteenth-century philosophy of Descartes
(Descartes summarized this in the oft-quoted aphorism 'I
think therefore I am' and presumably would never have said
'I feel therefore I am'). In line with this split, the mind has
often been associated with having a more male quality.
Emotions and bodily elements have correspondingly often
been seen as more female. These distinctions have generally
been informed by misogynistic attitudes in patriarchal
cultures.

Another metaphor, strongly linked with what is said
above, is that emotions have also been viewed as somewhat wild forces that should be controlled. Part of what
the mind or rationality should be doing is controlling the
potentially dangerous and weakening feelings. Many of our
definitions of emotions reflect this openly. For example,
'emotionalism' is 'the habit of cultivating or of weakly
yielding to the emotions' (*Shorter Oxford English Dictionary*).
Controlling one's feelings is implicitly the important stance
to take.

Therapy has in many ways followed these ideas of emotion, and emotion has been correspondingly devalued in many types of therapy. Emotion is notably absent, particularly in the discourses of family therapy and brief therapy. Part of this lack of discussion about emotion may be a response to traditional counselling training which seemed only to reflect feelings; an approach which might be parodied as 'parroting'. There is also a concern that clients may get bogged down in problem talk and be lost in a mire of depression or anger. However, it has become apparent in our work that the focusing on emotions is highly significant and helpful. In practice it readily becomes apparent whether an exploration is enabling new emotional connections or whether it is just 'digging a deeper rut'.

It may also be part of a more traditionally 'male' orientation to writing about therapy, which favours instrumental language over affective. In line with this, the root metaphor of 'system', which underpinned family therapy for many years (cf. Hoffman, 1990, 1991) easily leads to non-emotional and mechanical descriptions of persons (as components of the system). Focusing on things like restraints of feedback and redundancy leads to exploration of patterns and information, but not of the emotional.

The most significant reason for devaluing emotion, however, may be linked to our views of what emotions are. If emotions are taken to be just the feelings someone has, then there may be little to say about them other than to demonstrate some empathy and understanding. There may in fact be a desire to get past this feeling talk as quickly as possible in order to get on with what is perceived to be the 'real' subject-matter of the therapy.

Our suggestion is that no single definition of emotion can really be valid. Attempts to tie 'emotions' tightly to one definition can easily be counterproductive. So far there has been a broad range of definitions, most of which locate emotions within the body, and almost all of which attempt to categorize emotions. Some examples: the James–Lang theory claims that: 'The bodily changes following directly the perception of the existing fact, and our feelings of the same changes as they occur IS the emotion' (James, 1884: 189). Put in another way: emotions are seen as physiological changes occurring after a stimulus. Several theorists have attempted to categorize emotions, making lists of a number of key emotions (such as anger, fear, surprise and so on), with other emotions being subsets or mixtures of them. Some have even spoken of emotions in terms of formulae. This was the case of Simonov (1970), who suggested that $E = N(I_n - I_a)$ where emotion = needs multiplied by the difference between the necessary information and the available information.

In what follows we want to claim that it is extremely useful to see emotions as moral and relational orientations. We want to draw attention to how people can be seen to be taking moral and relational positions when they are 'entering into' or changing emotional states and when they do 'emotion talk'. In doing this we will use different associations and metaphors. As an entry point we suggest considering emotion as 'embodied understanding' or 'embodied knowing' (Rosaldo, 1984). From this perspective ignoring emotional responses amounts to ignoring moral and relational stances people are taking. And we know that moral and relational issues are, of course, crucial elements in therapy.

Two brief examples may help to set a context. These examples of helpful 'emotion talk' are from therapy sessions of one of the authors (G.S.). They are not presented as particularly innovative or unusual interactions. What we see here is something which could commonly arise within therapy sessions. In the first interaction a mother, father and 20-year-old son were involved in a first session of counselling. They were particularly concerned about the hostility and number of fights between the son, James, and the father, Don. Additional concerns were the father's drinking and James' habit of getting into financial trouble, requiring his parents repeatedly to 'bail him out'.

Example 1   As they talked, Don and James became very angry with each other. Don was talking about how much he did for his son and James was interrupting, saying 'that's bullshit' and swearing at him. As they talked I [G.S.] was able to speak a bit more with James and ask about these things. He talked about being 'fed up' and extremely angry because of so many years of accusations and arguments and because what he'd done hadn't been acknowledged. He said no matter what he did it was wrong. I asked him, 'When are the times that you can express some of your hurt or your disappointment as hurt and disappointment, rather than having it come out as anger?' After this question the tone of the session changed. His reply was 'not often', but spoken in a very soft, almost sighing, manner. The heat of the interaction diminished. There was a sense of much more openness. He became much more self-reflective. This opened the way for quite different types of discussion to emerge. Don and James were able to talk about their disappointments, their desire for more closeness, those times they had felt closer and how they might interact differently in the future.

In the second case a stepfather, Jim, and stepdaughter, Julie, had also been engaged in many fights and arguments.

Example 2   Julie said that Jim was mean, that he was uncaring, unfair and 'out to get' her. He said that she was rebellious and always wanted to provoke him, that she was always in trouble and didn't care about anyone else but herself.

In exploring the history of their relationship, I was able to ask each of them if they had ever had any secret hopes for closeness in their relationship. There was a silence and then some tentative acknowledgement that this was indeed the case. There was a shift of the emotional tone of the session. Then Jim and Julie could both talk about how each of them had felt rejected and disappointed about the way they had not been able to establish closeness together. When this happened we could begin to talk of how they might work together, how their disappointment might not get in the way and what it might mean if they could both recognize that they had each held and lost some of this hope. There was a sense of closeness and potential for change.

In these interactions talking about emotions led to significant changes, far beyond just changing a label of a feeling. However, in the above examples we could also see a naming of a feeling in the traditional sense – people do feel things in typical ways and we can name those experiences. But the naming doesn't account for enough. Emotions can clearly also be seen as processes that are better understood in a context of culturally defined notions of morality, relationships and power.

Emotion and culture

One way of entering this domain is to draw upon anthropological work. Geoffrey White has looked at processes of emotion talk in a Solomon Island society (White, 1990). According to him emotions are embedded in complex understandings about identities and scenarios of action, especially concerning the sorts of events that evoke the emotion, the relationships within which the event has taken place, and the responses expected to follow from it. These understandings can be seen as part of a generalized model of each emotion. Talk of a specific emotional response implicitly characterizes an action or event as an instance of a general type. In most cultures a limited number of key emotions impose such generalized understandings. So, the emotions can be seen to be a form of relational knowledge.

White drew on the work of Catherine Lutz (1987) to suggest that we can represent emotional schemas in the following form:

$$\text{social event}$$
$$\downarrow$$
$$\text{emotion}$$
$$\downarrow$$
$$\text{action response}$$

In talking about anger[7] we can see a model implying that there is (1) a perceived transgression by the other party (someone has done something wrong), (2) that there is a response to that of anger which (3) implies or demands a response of some type of retribution or recompense. If we talk about sadness or hurt what we have is (1) an implication of damage having been done to a close relationship, which (2) elicits an emotional response of hurt, and (3) the response invited by that hurt or sadness (an invitation for some type of repair of the relationship).

In each of these feeling scenarios we can see that there has been some sort of breach of the relationship. The anger leads to a sense of needed retribution. Hurt suggests an implied desire for closeness or at least a recognition of a desire for closeness:

[handwritten annotations: "reorganize", "relational knowledge →relationships", "terms used define reality of situation"]

transgression/wrong-doing   breach of close relationship

↓   ↓ *[handwritten: "understanding"]*

anger   hurt *[handwritten: "orientation perspective"]*

↓   ↓

recompense/retribution   repair relationship

We can see that often in talking about what has happened between people it is very often possible to talk about different emotions in relation to the same situation. The different feeling terms reflect different understandings of the situation and people's relationships, as in:

[7] We follow White's analysis where he explores a process of 'disentangling' occurring within the Solomon Islands society of Santa Isabel. He describes the Santa Isabel emotion *di'a tagna*, which he translates as anger. It follows the prototypical schema: transgression–anger–retribution. He says that this emotion implies a moral breach. It is only appropriate within certain relationships. It is not appropriate in this culture between a parent and child, but can be appropriate, for example, between mature men of relatively equal status. White contrasts this emotion with an alternative emotion of *di'a nagnafa*, which he translates as sadness. This also follows a prototypical schema. Whereas talk of anger constitutes a challenge to the other person and implies a demand for retribution, talk of sadness emphasizes reconciliation and relatedness.

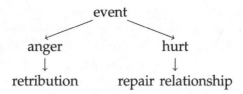

Of course, this is not to deny the naming of the 'feeling' the person had at a particular time, but there is rarely a sense of 'pure' feeling – the anger may be associated with frustration or hurt or a sense of being slighted or rejected etc. If naming other feelings 'connects' or feels true for the person it opens different possibilities. Emotions in this way can be clearly seen as embodied understandings, particularly if we remember Wittgenstein's sense of understanding as knowing 'how to go on'. Each emotion implies a different sense of how to go on.

Emotion, hierarchy, evaluation

A significant related point is that emotion and talk about emotions has important implications for social hierarchy. Each emotion implies a certain position or movement in the moral order.

Anger often implies that the person being angry is moving to a position of more power in relation to the other person. An army sergeant speaking with a private could be an illustration of this. If the sergeant tells the private that he/she is doing lousy work and needs to sharpen up, the latter will in most cases probably think little of it – in most cases the private would try to perform a bit better. If the private were to say the same thing to the sergeant, the sergeant would probably be furious because of the breach of the power relationship. The private being reproached will not get angry because the reproach occurs within the accepted power relationship and does not lower his already lower status (he/she might instead feel dejected, dis-acknowledged or resentful).

In arguments like that between Don and James in Example 1 above, the anger expressed implicitly demands the other to be 'one-down'. Talk of hurt on the other hand implies an experienced equal footing in the relationship. This allows more possibility for resolution without loss of face or status.

Emotional experience is always informed by our relational status in the local moral order – emotions are partly evaluative stances or orientations. Because of this emotional talk is also moral talk. Emotions can be seen as a form of embodied moral knowledge, knowledge about what is happening in a relationship.

Anger and hurt are of course only two examples of emotions with immense social implications. The practical implications of remorse, for example, are very important in the judicial system. If a person is convicted of a crime the question of whether or not they show remorse is often important in determining the sentence they will get. A folk model of remorse might be described in the following way: realization of having done wrong leads to feeling of remorse and implied future action of retribution, or at least changed behaviour. The model implies accepting a lower position in the local moral order from which the person can work towards regaining status, as they make recompense or demonstrate change.

It should be clear throughout this discussion that the types of emotion we describe and feel are largely socially constructed. The understandings of moral worth, relative positions in local hierarchies, and what constitutes offence or neglect or reparation are all cultural constructs. While there may be feelings, such as fear of physical danger, which are possibly common across all cultures, most of our emotions are about acculturated understandings. The types of emotions we feel and describe also have strong gender links: we are acculturated differently as men and women. In patriarchal cultures anger, for example, is more readily accepted in men than women, because of its implications for status and hierarchy (see Smith, 1992b).

Emotion, discourse and motivation

When speaking about difficulties and problems people tend to become more restricted in the voices they can access. Feeling cornered often leads to sticking more and more rigidly to some moral views and positions. In many cases only the voices of defensiveness can be accessed. In these kinds of situations people often use words without any consciousness of their touching and emotion-eliciting capabilities. They think that they are only 'describing' facts. All this is even more true about expert-languages in helping practices, which intend to appear to be totally representational: in most extreme cases professionals find it odd if somebody tells them that something they say could create conflicts between people or depress and discourage them.

What is needed in situations of stuckness is a way of helping people explore different voices again. This can happen through the processes of validation and through recognition of different emotions, motives and goals.

Different ways of speaking of emotions open the way to particular types of discourse and narrative. Talk about feeling depressed could work as an illustration: this kind of talk tends to be personalized, intrapsychic and devaluing. The 'depression' is situated 'inside' and there are often references to popular psychodynamic discourse. If a person feels angry, she is more likely to see herself as acting in relation to something. There is often a sense of moving forward or a sense of possibly being able to regrade herself. In anger-talk there is also usually reference to interaction and other people.

For depressed persons a move to anger-talk creates new options. It opens the possibility of seeing things interactionally, of regrading themselves, of seeing themselves as being victims of wrong-doing (as opposed to not deserving any better). The movement from intrapsychic to interactional is taken even further if we look at outrage. Outrage is very rarely seen as something within the person. Outrage is typically something someone feels about an injustice; 'It is an outrage that this could have happened'. It is the event which is taken to be outrageous and the implication is that any decent person would find it so.

It is often extremely useful to show that people (from another perspective) have been acting out of good intentions. Because of this it is important for the therapist/interviewer/helper to look for <u>signs of moral accomplishment and self-care</u> in practically everything clients do and say. Even the most sinister sounding descriptions of blaming, incapability, failure, or the most extreme self-criticism can in most cases be seen to contain at least a grain of successful coping, heroism or altruism.

Changes of emotion imply different manners of understanding, different tones, different moral and relational orientations. We can with good grounds claim that emotion largely determines the manner of our reasoning. Vygotsky (1986) suggested that when looking at the complex inter-relationships of thought and language, we must conclude that the superior authority is not thought that begets thought, or language which begets thought, but our 'affective volitional tendencies'.

Jerome Bruner (1990) has discussed the role of affect in relation to narrative accounts of memory, by drawing on the work of Bartlett (1932):

> He insists in remembering that what is most characteristic of 'memory schemata' as he conceives them is that they are under the control of an affective 'attitude'. Indeed, he remarks that any 'conflicting tendencies' likely to interrupt individual poise or to menace social life are likely to destabilize memory organization as well. It is as if unity of affect (in contrast to 'conflict') is a condition for economical schematization of memory . . .
> Indeed, Bartlett goes further than that. In the actual effort to remember something, he notes, what most often comes first to mind is an affect or a charged 'attitude' – that 'it' was something unpleasant, something that led to embarrassment, something that was exciting. The affect is rather like a general thumbprint of the schema to be reconstructed. The recall is then

a reconstruction made largely on the basis of this attitude, and its general effect is that of a justification of the attitude. (Bruner, 1990: 58)

For clients in therapy a change in emotional posture is usually linked with changes in what they are open to discuss, recognize and remember in relation to themselves or their relationships. By helping to open a new 'emotional state', they can be helped to create space to explore new meanings and possibilities. Attending to the changing emotional tone of a session can thus be extremely helpful.

Emotion-talk has also significant implications regarding people's motivation. 'Motivation' and 'emotion' come in fact from the same root words. Emotion implies a motion or movement. According to the *Shorter Oxford English Dictionary* the word 'emotive' stems from the Latin *emovere* from *e-* (ex; from) and *movere* (move) implying movement out of or moving forth (as 'evoke' is a calling forth). Emotive is defined as 'causing movement'. 'Motivation' also derives from the Latin word for movement and is defined in terms of that which induces a person to move or act. So etymologically the link between emotive and motive – or emotion and motivation – is clear. The *Shorter OED* also lists the word 'emove' , now rare, which means 'to move (to an action) or to excite emotion in'. In day-to-day life we implicitly acknowledge this link. Often when we talk of someone's motivation we do that in feeling terms. We can say, for example, that they acted out of love or resentment or fear.

If we talk with people about their feelings, we are often implicitly commenting on their motivations. So with Jim and Julie (Example 2 on p. 131), commenting on their disappointment at not having their secret hopes for closeness realized enabled a change in their interaction. They could now re-evaluate each other. They could see that each other's actions were not motivated by hatred or malice but were motivated at least in part by disappointment and a felt sense of rejection. In being able to rejudge the

feelings ~ motivations

motivation they could also make a different judgement of the identity of the person that they were speaking to.

It is important to notice that we should be interested also in the mobilizing forces of therapists and schools of therapy. Narrative therapists, for example, seem frequently to draw upon some definite metaphors, one of which is 'fight'. Clients are often invited to think about their situation through questions related to protest, to standing up against an injustice or fighting something oppressive. Even if the fight is against abstract things, people make emotional shifts when they move away from a submissive stance. It is helpful to have several basic metaphors for the relationships between clients and problems. Through them we can notice what acts as a mobilizing force for the person. It could be many things. Experiences like courage, needs for closeness, a desire to belong, beauty, a sense of mystery or curiosity are also common descriptions of mobilizing factors.

Different metaphorical descriptions of passions and mobilizing forces can both connect and separate clients and therapists. The capability to be mobilized by something and not by something else forms an interface between them, there has to be at least some overlap of passions and motivating forces for cooperation to work. Some therapists seem to be free to move between a few of these different mobilizing forces; some are able or prefer to stick to only one.[8]

Recognition of the possibility of different descriptions of emotional experience allows for new possibilities for people who feel stuck in one particular emotion and correspondingly with one particular moral-relational position. Billig's ideas of the dilemmatic nature of thinking, Bakhtin's notions about dialogism, Derrida's (and Adorno's) distinction between identity logic and supplementary logic and Shotter's views of relational and anticipatory knowledge all

---

[8] One may be reminded here of Milton Erickson's ideas on therapy (e.g. Haley, 1973). Erickson said repeatedly that the words and techniques are unimportant. What is important is enlisting people's motivation.

tie in with the notion of emotional difference. What all these ideas imply is the heterogeneity of perspectives and the fact that it is always possible to illuminate only some things at any one time. Different emotion definitions and emotion words allow different possibilities of many kinds. People can become aware of views obscured or marginalized by each way of speaking, thinking and imagining, and so also of different elements of their experience, of different potentials and possibilities.

It is, of course, not credible to claim that an angry person is feeling happy, excited or overjoyed. Many other descriptive options are still available, but the experience and the description of it will mutually influence each other. An analogy could be found in sculpting. The type of wood, stone or metal may partly determine the type of product that can be made. The process of chiselling it, and the tools used, may influence that too. In the end you cannot say that the finished product is entirely due to the materials, or entirely due to the types of tools used, nor entirely due to the person operating upon it. Somehow all of these things are inextricably interwoven. The attempt to find names and descriptions for emotions also relates to values and social acceptability, and with the construction of narratives which allow a sense of moral worth. People try to find names and categories which are acceptable and understandable for themselves and for others.

The task is also future-oriented. To talk about emotions is to talk not only about what people have felt. We know that names or classifications of emotional states affect the future of relationships. If we know someone's feelings, we know both the direction they are setting out in, and where they are setting out from.

Strong and consistent emotions can be experienced as confining or imprisoning. People can feel locked inside of sadness or rage or frustration. They can also be locked inside something which does not at first sight look like emotion at all, such as coldness or indifference. Sometimes when people lose a sense of freedom or flow regarding emotions a very minor thing can make all the difference. Even if someone is feeling totally flat or empty, we often find that there are moments when they smile or laugh. They can also express irritation about something. There are moments when they sigh deeply, moments when they breathe more subtly – there are all sorts of fluctuations and combinations of emotions occurring all the time. It is relatively easy to draw attention to this flux and multiplicity. Indeed, we can consider <u>any conversation as being a continual interplay, change and flux of orientations.</u>

Simply being alert to this flux opens many possibilities. A further brief example may illustrate this:

Example 3 The family had a long history of fighting and antagonism between the mother and the teenage son. At one moment they talked about a time of being more cooperative. I asked them what they noticed about their relationship then. They were able to talk about this friendship and cooperation. As they did this, a sense of warmth developed in the session. When speaking about this feeling they could talk about warmth in their relationship in general – when that was more visible, what they noticed about it etc. In doing this the definition of their relationship changed.

The previous discussion makes it understandable that there are some common things which rigidify negative motivational interpretations. If somebody perceives a person as being more powerful, then he/she is considered more likely to impart negative intentions. If the person seen as more powerful does something problematic to others (keeps a distance, makes strange comments, or whatever) it is hard to experience her/him as acting out of defensiveness or vulnerability. On the other hand, if the other person is seen as being more vulnerable or disempowered, it is very easy to accept the idea that many of their actions with negative consequences are based on forgivable misunderstandings or misconstruals. If vulnerability is seen, the people around that person often become softer in their approaches. The recognition of vulnerability in a social setting is also often followed by a general feeling of increased freedom: if others are seen as being vulnerable, people can also allow themselves to be vulnerable.

For similar reasons it is often helpful to talk about dreams and goals. Parents and teenagers who feel stuck can talk about how the parents want to help the teenager achieve some particular goal. The goal could be achieving independence, or not to be hurt like their parents were, or to be able to be strong or close to others.

It is important to notice that reconceptualizations of goals and motives do not necessarily follow questions. The main source of these shifts probably lies in the responses to clients' utterances. As Bakhtin tells us, the meaning of the word or utterance becomes apparent from the response. Another way to say this is that every dialogue is *also* a dialogue about motives, methods and goals. Whatever the other party says, she/he either supports or transforms the views of motives, paths of action and goals expressed or implied in what has been said previously.

To be useful, dialogues about goals, paths and motives should aim at descriptions that can resonate for every participant. These descriptions can, for example, concern a shared hope, sadness, curiosity, longing, commitment, excitement or grief. We are thus looking for words, stories, labels and expressions that everyone can agree to look through. What is reached in successful moments is a feeling of all participants reaching and touching something together. What we are talking about here are the unordered, half-formed, yet-to-be-specified feelings and experiences that some expressions and words can represent.

Finally, we cannot *not* be in movement when we are interacting, or not be in action, and these processes, qualities, tones, evaluative reactions are part of every conversation and every speech turn. We cannot ignore them without losing the sense of the conversation. It is, you could say, like trying to analyse a symphony by only describing the instruments. Responding to these types of movements or *e*-moving elements is especially crucial in all forms of therapy because it opens up immediate possibilities for different understandings of motivation, relational positions, different narratives, different discourses, and different moral evaluations. Traditional views of emotion tend to obscure all of this.

Emotion and definition of self

Emotion words we use are important in defining persons and also in self-definitions – emotions and qualities of character are closely linked. Many emotional descriptions of people (e.g. a kind person, a warm person, a jealous person, an angry person, a person filled with sadness) are linked with definitions of identity. This opens many new potentials for therapeutic interaction. We offer one further example: a counselling session with a mother, Jennifer, and her three children.

Example 4 Jennifer was talking about her eldest son, David, who was 14, and his deep-seated, destructive jealousy. When his younger sister came home from hospital after being born ten years ago, he had tipped her out of the pram. There were descriptions of his jealousy having been there continually since then. I [G.S.] asked them what things were like when the brother and sister got on better together. As they began to discuss that, there was a change of emotional tone. Everybody began to talk about times of playing together. While the type of question is a common one within either a solution-focused or narrative model, these types of emotional changes are not so often described in solution-focused or narrative vignettes . . . David's mother changed her tone from being hostile and derisive towards her son. When I asked her what things were like for the two of them when they were getting on better she could say they have quite a bit of fun when things were going well, that they often sit and play computer games or cards together. She then went on to say laughingly that she thought a lot of their problems could be solved if her son wasn't so addicted to the TV set. From that point we started working on the TV addiction rather than the deep-seated, lifelong jealousy, and they were able to make quite rapid changes. The shift to a warmer, laughing, humorous tone is very much an emotional shift, and this emotional shift is what was most significant in the session. It does not necessarily follow in any strictly 'rational' way from just finding exceptions to the jealousy. The change of tone created the possibility for quite different 'jumps' of thinking. It clearly opened different potentials for discussion and interaction. Different types of memories also became more readily available. In turn, different descriptions of David's sense of fun and his qualities as a 'big brother' and friend began to emerge.

Recurrent or predominant emotions or moods are especially important regarding the maintenance of identities. This is often clearly visible with people suffering from depression. As we have seen previously, in most cases it is relatively easy to describe a range of other feelings which relate to the dominant one. Each emotion term also opens the way to different understandings of self. Seeing the element of hurt implies that caring or commitment has been frustrated. Describing the experience as despair, implies that the despair may be linked with a persistence which has gone unrewarded. Both these views could allow a regrading of self. During the process of exploring alternative descriptions and definitions of feelings people will develop more choice over their self-identity or the identity of their relationships.

6
Living Conversations

Expand our languages, all of them, demands Cortazar; free them from habit, or amnesia, or silence, turn them into a dynamic, all-inclusive metaphor that admits all our verbal forms – impure, baroque, conflictive, syncretic, polycultural.
(Carlos Fuentes, 1995: 60)

Savo style

One of the districts of Finland is Savo. The people living there are famous for their innumerable proverbs and for the indirectness of their speech. In a way they are specialists in responding in ways which transform the questions posed by others. Some could say that they are smart-asses. They would not deny that. They would (perhaps) say: 'Yes, isn't it good to have two smart ends?' – or 'Perhaps you are right'.

These people generally detest both questions that are too direct and answers that are easy or predictable. Why? Nobody knows. Their own explanation is that 'they simply have too curved jaws to speak straight'. A somewhat wider, but less Savo-style explanation, would be that these people hate dead, non-relational words. They make everything into a relational and inspirational matter. They like to say: 'Perhaps it will be, perhaps not'. They would perhaps like what we have written – or perhaps not.

per · extra, another
haps ~ happening
event, context.

Seeking shared signs of promise

A: You know I have been wondering more and more about the usefulness of research on dialogues. I mean, if the intent is to develop better practices.

B: You weren't so pessimistic about a year ago.

A: No. It's just that nowadays it seems so limiting to study some elements or units of interaction. The focus is always in the fixed meaning of something . . . word or sentence or whatever. But if we are in a conversation ourselves it is different . . . it is not the fixed meaning, it is the <u>interplay.</u>

x-sectional moment

B: This relates to the differences between language as it is written and language in the speaking.

A: Yes. Really important things cannot be explained by only looking at one something at a time. They are matters of moment, of being in something. Consider the dance metaphor. The success or beauty of a dance cannot be evaluated by studying the steps of one of the partners. So the <u>focus should not be on what people say,</u> but <u>in how the things they say interact or dance with each other.</u>

B: So what does this kind of research look like then?

A: That is the big question. Most of the methods are so crude. We could study . . . let's say thematic continuity, or interruptions of themes and narratives by the participants, or asymmetries . . . amount of speech time for participants, or the ways some people dominate the choice of topics. But this leaves out things like feelings of meaningfulness or recognition . . . and intimacy, playfulness and trust.

B: So, do you have any ideas about what to do?

A: Some glimpses . . . perhaps. You know, I can show somebody a video-taped session where everything runs nicely . . . there is progress, good atmosphere, trust, intimacy etc. And then I ask the audience how all this is produced – and they cannot tell. Of course, they can always say something . . . So, I am afraid the methods are missing and will be missing forever. It is the local knowledges, <u>knowledge of the third kind</u> which matters.

3rd Kind

B: How do you think about teaching therapy skills then?

A: That is a big question, too. First, I think really good training can happen only in small and intimate groups. Maybe four, five people. It has to include many things. Sensitivities to meta-phoricality and tones of interaction and talk, listening skills, openness to feedback, skills of friendly interpretations, focusing on connectedness, all kinds of consultative approaches, poetic thinking. Lots of things. I also think it has to really connect to the lives of the trainees themselves. It cannot just be training in techniques of what to do with others. The most important thing might be to remember that the whole thing is craft-work, all situations are unique. The timespans of those things and activities, whatever they are, which maintain promise and intimacy can be very short. It's mostly about the knowledge of the third kind. But we are used to thinking on a long-term basis. We see knowing as knowing the same thing forever.

B: Do you think then that therapy conversations should be some kind of poetry?

A: I think they always are, in a way. But often they are very bad poetry. But I also think the view of therapy as art shouldn't be advertised too much. Many people have difficulties with these kinds of words. A colleague of mine hates the word 'art', for example. He thinks art is just consumerism nowadays. He would like people to do art and stop talking about it in fancy ways.

B: I remember you have talked a lot about resources previously. You don't mention them at all now.

A: I don't know why I talk less of them. Maybe it is just getting tired with the word. Maybe it is somehow difficult to connect it to the potential nature of things which are useful. The word 'resource' somehow concretizes things. I use expressions like 'signs of shared promise' quite a lot now. I really think that it is signs of promise we should be hunting for together. This expression hints at the potential nature of things we are looking for.

B: Does it really?

A: For me it does. And I think promise really is a feeling, a felt invitation to think in certain ways. It can be difficult to see things like that from texts or transcripts. But anyway I think it's important to see that the providence or promise . . . or whatever we call it . . . is not in the words, it is in the use, in the orientation. The most difficult thing is that it is also social. I mean, in Bakhtin's sense. We always have this living context around us.

B: So, you cannot study texts and show how a certain specific promising word or idea is found or created.

A: I am not sure of that. In a way I think we can. But we have to look closely at the non-verbal things. We feel it in the air . . . I just had an idea. We could take one transcription and one video tape and go through them and see what happens. I have a good one here on the shelf. We have the necessary permissions.

B: OK. What is it about? Why do think it is good?

A: Let's see. The interview took place here. The client is a young woman who has recently finished school. She is thinking about further studies. Her main complaint is bulimia. The session is the second . . . or third . . . in a series of five or six with the same therapist. She is happy for us to use it. I think the session represents her normal style. I was part of a team for the session. What more could I say? The client is quite shy but also smiles quite easily. She has a good sense of humour and obviously likes to have fun. It is summer . . .

B: How about the atmosphere?

A: The interview has a good atmosphere, a very good atmosphere, there is lots of smiling, some laughter . . . and yet it is not easy to say why the atmosphere is so constructive. I have seen it several times and always wondered where all the good humour comes from. So, this can be a kind of test case. I think we should first read the transcripts and then look at the tape. I mean, immediately after reading, so we have a fresh memory of the text and of how it felt. It takes 5–10 minutes to read it.

B: You have copies of the transcript?

A: Yes. We have used it for training. I have two copies here. Does this sound OK to you?

B: Yes . . . it's fine with me.

(*A and B read the transcript. Ten minutes pass.*)

A: Ready?

B: Yep . . .

(*A and B watch the video tape.*)

Fine shoes: A client session

Client: *Hi!*

Therapist: *Hi!*

C: (smiles)

T: *You have got a pair of fine new shoes.*

C: *(smiles) When I was in (the client names her home town) my sister said that I can't buy these. She said that they were a terrible pair of shoes. Then I bought them. I don't like them that much but . . .*

T: *I think they are quite nice. I noticed them at once. Well . . . How has your summer been?*

C: *Quite good . . . or I've had a lot of good days.*

T: *Oh. Tell me a little about that.*

C: *Or something like that . . . there has been a few sort of . . . well, a period of three or four days.*

T: *Oh. Well done. I was . . . it is a funny thought, but when I saw those shoes of yours I thought that you must have had good days . . . I somehow associated in my mind . . .*

C: *You did? I bought these when I was in (. . .), when was that? I was there in the beginning of July and at the end of June. It was July when I was with my sister. We spent two weeks together. It went really well.*

T: *Really!*

C: *When . . . Well first when I arrived . . . what . . . I was eating all the time and she got really angry and said that you are not allowed to do that. Even if I said that I would buy some for her too. She said no . . . that now we are going to make a deal that . . . that we are going to have our own food.*

T: *Good. So you stayed for two weeks with your sister in (. . .) is that so? And it went well?*

C: *It went really well. She bought food for herself and I bought food for myself. And then well . . . it was terribly good when . . . I realize that . . . or I have been sort of thinking . . . what I take . . . or what it is like . . . what doesn't so easily cause that binge eating fit. Well then I realized that if I eat healthy food, which is really sensible, that I don't eat only because I feel like it but because it is good for me . . . and I succeeded quite well at it. And then when she had her own food I didn't have any of those temptations that I always have when I'm home.*

T: *Exactly. By the way how do you explain how you managed those two weeks? How did that period go so well?*

C: *It didn't go that well all the time but I had . . . a couple of periods. And now I have also had . . . This is the third time now.*

T: *Well this is quite . . . yes (answers intercom call) . . . What they wanted to ask and make explicit over there is what do you think that it says about the nature of your problem that you have recently had so many good periods? What does it say to you about the nature of the problem?*

C: *I have been thinking that now I'm . . . I feel I've been in a way . . . Now things are beginning to go in a better direction.*

T: *Good. What has made you go towards that direction?*

C: *Well . . . I think that the biggest reason is that I've got a motivation. I am somehow motivated.*

T: *Where has that come from . . . motivation?*

C: *Well it is hard to explain but I think it has got a lot to do with the fact that I moved here. That I am concretely alone and responsible for my own life.*

T: *How is it . . . how do you see that it has increased your motivation moving here and being alone?*

C: *Somehow that . . . I can't accuse anyone else. Now I realize that I couldn't have done that . . . there it would have been impossible to have good days like this because . . . By the way I'm going there today.*

T: *Where?*

C: *To (. . .).*

T: *I see.*

C: *I regret it a little and I'm scared because things have never, not ever gone well there. Maybe one day maximum. Because there it is always like . . . we always have our meals together and there is all the time all kinds of food in the pantry . . . and I visit our granny and she is all the time offering goodies. It's sick. For some foreigners it is peculiar that here people are fed all the time. But I can't. But here I can organize my life so that . . . well . . . there are no situations with risk . . . they don't come up.*

T: *And you know how you should do that? It's quite . . . A lot of people don't necessarily know that.*

C: *Well I know how to do that in a way. At least if I am . . . first . . . if there is sort of a good day then I stay . . . it helps if I don't go anywhere . . . that I stay inside all day.*

T: How come?

C: Well I don't see any food. And well . . . Always when I go to a shop there is always a danger. The biggest danger of all is that when a binge eating fit begins . . . a sort of . . . I think it is a meal.

T: A family meal?

C: Yes.

T: That it is like a minefield?

C: Yes. I'm going to refuse completely.

T: Do you think that it is possible to do that?

C: I tell them, I even lie to them, that I'm on a diet, because on the other hand there at home it disgusts me. Well now . . . I try to eat well or something . . . when I feel like vomiting on the other hand it . . . that they all the time stare at what I eat. It's awful. That . . . now I'm independent when it comes to food. That . . . at least I don't start eating because somebody . . . that I'd have my revenge on our mother or something like that.

T: You have noticed that . . . ?

C: Yes, when I'm here.

T: Well do you have a feeling now that . . . you said that . . . or actually you already said that you've got a feeling that now you are going . . . that now the situation starts to get better. In a way does it mean that as long as you are here in Helsinki . . . or live independently . . . take care of your food? . . . How sure can you be that in the future . . . in a way under these circumstances . . . this thing will succeed? Fifty per cent is that it is only just and . . .

C: I don't know but I believe that . . . at least my motivation will stay high but . . . I'm sure I sometimes vomit and lapse. But I always want to try again.

T: Exactly. So you've got a feeling that the motivation will remain?

C: Yes.

T: What makes you trust that . . . that here you've got the motivation . . . ?

C: *Well somehow . . . when I'm there I don't have any other life than my family. I can't see any reason to try. But when I'm here alone . . . well now . . . there it is easy for me to completely stop thinking about the future so that I just eat. But here when I'm alone . . . somehow . . .*

T: *It's your own life.*

C: *Yes . . . that all my studies are my responsibility . . . and I can't think the same way at home . . . well I'm not going to think about anything when they are complaining about things. I can't really explain but somehow . . . And I guess that what is most important is that I now I . . . am capable myself. When some people said to me that . . . when I was working for young people in (. . .) . . . that youth organizer said . . . when she heard that I still lived at home . . . she said that because I was grown up it would be good if I were to live elsewhere. I didn't really understand it until now. The most crucial thing is that I'm living alone.*

T: *Exactly. Well what else do you think . . . you actually have already described quite a lot but is there still something that maintains this motivation here? What kind of inclinations or things of yours maintain it?*

C: *Well very little things. One can imagine that when I get into a vicious circle of binge eating . . . what kinds of things I can be happy about when I don't have this bulimia. For example, now I listen to the radio. I don't have time to listen to the radio when I am eating and vomiting. I watch the telly. And go to the movies. When I've got that binge eating period I don't allow myself to go to the movies because I can't fully enjoy the movie. Half of the time I'm anyhow thinking about the food. Then I call a friend of mine on the phone a lot and . . . go to the library.*

T: *Does this friend of yours live here or in your home town?*

C: *In my home town.*

T: *And you keep in touch there?*

C: *And with another one too that lives in (. . .). So that I have all kinds of other things. So that . . . I feel kind of peaceful and don't think about the food all the time.*

T: So in my opinion you are describing quite a lot of what you were hoping when we met last time and what you were looking for. It seems that you have really succeeded in that . . . in achieving that. Well, do you think these are connected, this motivation and so on . . . so what else do you think this kind of period makes possible when eating doesn't take . . .

C: It makes everything possible . . . so that . . . well . . . That binge eating and vomiting lowers one's self-esteem . . . that somehow I begin to think that I can't do anything and it is useless to try. Now, by the way, I have found . . . I haven't told you I'm going to move away from the lady's place. In the beginning of September I'm going to get a lovely one-room flat in (. . .) for a year.

T: That's nice.

C: Yes.

T: Did you look for a rental flat yourself or was it by pure chance?

C: I noticed it in a newspaper.

T: Nice.

C: I looked at quite a few and I already thought that no . . . Well a sort of normal life or somehow I feel that . . . Somehow I feel safe when I think . . . It often comes to my mind when some people say that one must have some basic security in one's life and some people believe in something and so on. I think that if I can eat normally . . . it is enough for basic security.

T: Have you noticed at this point . . . when you talked quite a lot about liking oneself . . . that somehow it was related to this theme of how you have experienced things?

C: It is miraculous that it still can change from that when I am always so low in self-esteem. I mean that I am really pleased with myself now.

T: What . . . from what kind of things do you notice that?

C: For example I . . . this sounds really superficial and is that too . . . but it is really important for me that my face looks terrible when I vomit. I really look as if I had mumps and my eyelids puff up and everything. And now I don't look swollen and it's wonderful . . . And then one thing . . . my . . . my front teeth have gone really terribly worn out and everything like that so

... I have an appointment with a dentist and my father has promised that they can loan me the money then ...

T: Exactly. So that you think that it is ... ?

C: Well, then when I've got ... for example a week ago when I had another binge eating thing so ... or I had some of those bad days ... It is terribly important ... or ... it is not that important ...

T: Exactly. Well ... (telephone call) Yes. Well I want to return to this same theme ... that you are now quite confident in this ... and you've got your own life here ... and you feel that you have got a hold of it and you have got ways to function here but this danger zone comes up when you go there ...

C: That's right.

T: ... to your home ... and you already told me a little, that you have been thinking how to make that danger smaller. That you have already thought about refusing to take part in these family meals. Have you got any other ideas about what could make your visits home a bit better? What could help in that? ... Actually ... I interrupt you a little ... you must have visited there after we talked with your parents?

C: I visited there the next day ... no I can't remember. Maybe so. No ... I went there the day before.

T: Did you discuss anything about it? Did it come up in some way?

C: No they only said that: 'Yes we went there.'

T: I see.

C: They didn't tell me what you had talked about.

T: And you didn't ask any more questions?

C/T: (Laughter)

T: OK ... but let's go back to this theme about what one could do.

C: Well that has at least helped me that ... well ... now I have defined myself so that ... I can eat only healthy food ... so that I don't again ... because I'd like to get back the original contact to food ...

T: You want to eat healthy food?

C: *Yes, and nothing else. Because if I eat something else I feel that I'm doing something wrong and then . . .*

T: *I see. Well how can this then come true? How are you then going to carry this out in your home town?*

C: *Well I have thought that I won't eat those meals. I'll buy food for myself.*

T: *Yes. Well what do you think . . . will it go without pain or will it become . . . ?*

C: *I'm very uncertain.*

T: *But do you think that if they will say something you will be able to carry out your plan? How certain do you feel about that?*

C: *Quite uncertain or . . . This friend of mine that has got anorexia . . . if I have good days in (. . .) . . . so . . . she gets really angry.*

T: *Who?*

C: *My friend. She is envious.*

T: *I see.*

C: *I was only thinking that is this delusion of persecution of mine . . . or something . . . but I anyway feel that it can't be only that because also my sister behaves the same way. She said that when I had this January . . . a good month . . . she told me afterwards, when things were not so good, that she was really envious of me then. That I was going out all the time and so on.*

T: *What were they envious of you about? About your going out?*

C: *This friend of mine hasn't said so . . . but somehow . . .*

T: *Exactly.*

C: *It is disgusting.*

T: *Yes. How do you experience . . . think about this envy then? On the other hand it can be a quite nice feeling that someone envies you, then you can think that as a matter of fact you are doing all right when someone envies you. But do you think that it is only a negative thing?*

C: *I think it's only negative.*

T: *Well how then when you are having those good days in . . . so what do you do in order to maintain them or to prolong them? . . . Is it a good idea to call this friend then or are you trying to avoid it or how do you see this thing?*

C: Well I didn't really want to see her then . . . but . . . my sister even if she said herself that she was envious . . . but anyhow I thought . . . I didn't pay that much attention to it . . . at least during the summer it didn't disturb me in any way. We had a really nice time . . . she gave me support.

T: That's nice. Yes. How much older is she?

C: Eighteen months.

T: Yes. (Intercom call) If a sort of ⌐miracle⌐ would happen now unexpectedly in (. . .) so that things would be different there, the situation would be good . . . and you would feel that you could carry out your plans and you would have a nice time there. What would be different then in your opinion? How would your parents behave? What would you do yourself? What would your sister do? And in what way would the <u>situation be different?</u>

C: Well it would be different in that way that . . . It would actually be more irritating because I get terribly irritated when . . . if I happen to have better times they treat me . . . like well . . . especially my mother and also . . . father he doesn't understand anything . . . but my mother goes at once like 'wonderful' and then she thinks that . . . that now I am almost her best friend . . . that now we can talk . . . and . . . that let's talk now about what it was like when things were not going so well for you. Disgusting. That my . . . when I vomit it is my own territory . . . that . . . I can stay away from others.

T: Exactly. (Intercom call) That actually the good situation would be in a way the situation would get out of hand . . . that you would have to do things in relation to your parents that you wouldn't want to do now?

C: When . . . what do you mean?

T: When on the other hand in a way the situation would be good for you.

C: Yes that's true. That's true. When things were going all right here I somehow realize that I . . . I am responsible about everything . . . and I do everything . . .

T: Now you are somehow . . . what would you hope that your mother would do? What would be a better alternative?

C: She wouldn't pay attention to the whole thing.

T: *She wouldn't say anything about it?*

C: *Yes. But I know that immediately when I go there she already has all the food . . . everything . . . hidden and then she has prepared a family meal. She puts on everyone's plate just a small . . . For some reason it irritates me a lot. But I've been thinking that now I'm going to tell her directly that I'm on a diet and that I eat healthy food only . . . and I don't eat this stuff. It goes quite well if . . . if I don't introduce myself so that they can't interpret it so that I can't eat normally . . .*

T: *Exactly. So that you don't have to express whether you are feeling well or not . . . but you can say that at this point you only fancy healthy food.*

C: *Yes.*

T: *Exactly. Well how . . . when we still talk about this situation at home following the miracle. Things would go really well there . . . and you'd even have fun so what would happen there then? What would your father possibly do? And your sister?*

C: *But I don't want that it would be fun there.*

T: *What would be good from your point of view?*

C: *That they wouldn't be there in (. . .) at all. I am irritated by the thought that . . . I've got a feeling that they want to keep me . . . not as a little girl but so close. That I don't even by accident think in a different way than they do or something like that.*

T: *Yes?*

C: *They said at once: 'When you move into your one-room flat we will come and see you with daddy. We can stay the night' (laughs).*

T: *Well how, now that you can put this so clearly . . . how do you think that it affects things that . . . when you are there, how do you think that you can stay strong there? What can you do about it? So that you say that you are on the diet. Is there something else that you could do? Or could you get an ally . . . could you get an ally from for example your sister? Could she help you in that? What could work?*

C: *. . . I think that . . . Well that I'd . . . externally behave the same way as before. I'd go to the shop and bring home some terrible plastic bags. That irritates them terribly. And I'd stay in my room and . . . I wouldn't talk to them a lot.*

T: *But you would know yourself that you are in the control of the situation but you would let them think that you are not?*

C: *Yes.*

T: *Exactly.*

C: *So that I'd buy, for example, mineral water . . .*

T: *Exactly. So that you could behave as if you had this problem but it wouldn't bind you?*

C: *Yes . . . because I've been doing it here and it has helped.*

T: *But that's a good idea.*

C: *Even though the first day goes better if I stay in my room. But if I for example . . . on the second day . . . go to Carrolls or McDonalds . . . something that I love to do . . . But I would as if . . . Almost every day now when I'm having a good day I go there . . . but I take only coffee or orange juice. And then I go to a department store and I buy some fruit or something like that. So . . . that as much as possible I try to do everything in a normal way*

T: *I have a feeling . . . I'm going to check that I understood this right. Does this mean that this functions as a sort of buffer, at least when it comes to your mother . . . this binge eating. That at once if things start going too well for you this closeness becomes intolerable for you?*

C: *Yes – that's right.*

T: *So does it function as a buffer so that you'd continue this plastic bag thing and then they would interpret it so that she's not doing so well but you would know yourself that you are not doing so badly?*

C: *That's true.*

(Telephone call, end of the session.)

After the session

A: *(switches off the video tape)* Well, that was something wasn't it? What I like most is the <u>constant consulting</u> with the client. She is the expert here. And as I said the atmosphere is very nice too. From only reading the transcript I think it would really be difficult to sense that special smiling and constructive quality . . . or atmosphere from it. Why do you look so serious?

[margin note: Client is Consultant]

B: I don't know . . . it's just that . . . *(long pause)* I feel that I have maybe lost something during recent years. It would be difficult for me to do some of the things the therapist does here. I am much more methodical, more straightforward, and ordered. Maybe this reminded me of that. Often when I see things I like . . . or which I think I should have been able to do or see, I get sad. Do you understand that? I don't.

A: I know the feeling. But I don't think it is so bad. I think it cannot be avoided. Like when you meet people and places which you would have liked to have known already. How could it be avoided?

B: Yes, you are right, I guess. I was thinking also of those providential objects we have been talking about. I think the shoes could be a good example of how a concrete object starts to become providential. They seem to open a sense of promise and link to something good almost from the first utterance . . . a sense of hope or promise. The therapist says that they are nice. A very direct compliment.

A: Another thing of this kind was the healthy food. The client saw lots of promise in healthy food. The therapist confirmed this . . . at least she did not argue against it. It could be a related thing. And then the therapist asked the client about her own explanations for success. This happens often in solution-focused and narrative approaches, but I don't think that people often ask these kinds of things in normal life.

B: There was really lots of solution-focused stuff . . . positive exceptions . . . positive development . . . miracles . . . I was just thinking of what you said before we started to look at the tape. You said something about promising things. I was just thinking that maybe that is the reason why solution-focused and narrative conversations are useful for the clients generally. Maybe they are kind of half-automatic methods for bringing promise to view. I mean, it is difficult to avoid that with all those questions on exceptions and preferred outcomes.

A: Yes, but only half-automatic. I think that promising things are mostly not there already . . . mostly they have to be dug out. There is lots of consultation here about potentially promising things and ideas.

B: It is quite strange but these kinds of topics really seem to create a much looser structure of talk. When we talk of promising things and pleasures and things like that it becomes easier to jump from almost anything to anything. It is interesting that the narrative or solution-focused approaches might enhance this, because the theories themselves are quite methodical, and don't seem to imply this.

A: There was a strange moment in the interview. At one moment both of them laugh but there is nothing directly humorous there. Maybe it is some kind of an inside joke. It was about being indifferent to what her parents think.

B: Maybe she just enjoys not having to be interested in what her parents say or don't say.

A: The therapist does not seem to be at all interested in psychological things. Like envy. That is something people would not expect of psychological experts.

B: Yes, there were no comments of that kind . . . or maybe one. It also seemed to me that she was talking in a way which helped in somehow transforming the problem at home to some kind of play . . . the plastic bags and all. But the idea itself seemed to come from her, not from the therapist.

A: What does all this say about how to develop methods? Can these kinds of ideas and words . . . promising words . . . promising objects . . . be systematically produced?

B: I think so. I mean, as I just said certain kind of success and pleasure-orientated questions lead in that direction quite easily.

A: But it is not only questions of course?

B: Of course not. It is the atmosphere which kind of creates readiness to look at things in that light. And I think there really are many things which affect the atmosphere. As we have talked about before, the freedom to jump from whatever to whatever might be important. And a certain looseness of language. The looseness creates the feeling that we can have these more metaphorical senses of things. The conversation does not feel like an interrogation. You look lost in your thoughts?

A: Yes, I was thinking . . . I have been developing a secret theory . . . of a kind . . . during the last week or so, since I saw you last. It is quite crazy.

B: I like crazy theories . . . you know that.

A: But this is really crazy. It is about fluffiness . . . it is a theory of sixth or seventh dimension, the fluffy one.

B: You are right . . . that sounds crazy indeed. Please, I am dying to hear it . . . 'theory of fluffiness' . . . what a name!

A: It's not that spectacular. It is just that I think there are things which open and things which close . . . and that these two kinds of things don't exist in the same dimension.

B: Sounds really strange.

A: I agree. We all have lots of these small things and words which by being around make our lives more sparkling, lighter, more free, less rigid. Shoes for some, swallows for others . . . they can be whatever. And these things can change. They can come and go. And as we just saw, they can be created in talk. They are a counterforce to those things and words which pull us downwards.

B: Downwards in what sense?

A: Loss of vitality, depression, isolation . . . death, actually. These forces have perhaps something to do with Freud's Eros and Thanatos, except that I don't buy that instinctual stuff.

B: I find that quite acceptable. What you say about Freud is a little scary, though. But is it really so much words you are talking about.

A: I talk of words in Bakhtinian terms . . . very widely . . . but you are right, I refer to all kinds of things.

B: But what do you mean by saying that the two kinds of things are not in the same dimension? What is the dimension you are talking about?

A: That is the hard one. What do I mean? Let's take an indirect route. At least my best ideas often feel strangely light. You know the feeling? Suddenly you see something which is good. How did it happen? Often you smile and laugh a little. Where do these things really come from? What is common to them, I think, regardless of their type, is a certain kind of harmlessness and humorousness. They are light like summer clouds. The

happiness researcher, the American . . . I guess his name is Csik
. . . szent . . . mihalyi, I can never remember the name, talks of
'flow'. I think it comes quite close. What is this state of mind?
You feel that your ideas flow. There are no obstacles . . . no real
obstacles.

B: But the word 'dimension' . . . what do you mean by that?

A: I was coming to that . . . So, there are actually two realities
here, not one. I see that this has some relationship to what
Bakhtin was talking about when he spoke of centrifugal and
centripetal forces. In some of his texts he also contrasts an
'epic' orientation to a 'novelistic' one. When having an epic
orientation the authors or narrator are outside of what they are
narrating about. He then talks about finalized things, experiences, actions and happenings. A novel . . . I mean, a novel
defined in Bakhtinian manner . . . is open. Things and
characters are immersed in movement, in interaction. The
difference between these dimensions is, in a way, that
between a piece of argumentation and a piece of poetry,
or maybe better still, between a rigid and strictly figurative form
of art and playing with shapes and colours.

B: Now I start to see what you are trying to say.

A: I also just read something from Italo Calvino where he said that
he sometimes has had the feeling that the world is turning to a
stone. He sees it is the responsibility of writers to oppose this
process. Kundera has talked about the same responsibility in
several connections. I guess what I am saying is that the
dimensions of finalized and non-finalized things are really
different. And I think there really are many things which
obscure the existence of the non-finalized sphere.

B: Are these spheres related?

A: I don't think the one is a symmetrical opposite of the other. The
light or non-finalized cannot be extrapolated from the finalized.

B: What do you mean by that?

A: If you know a depressing thought, you cannot make any
deductions about what kind of light things would help to make
it disappear. There are actually two realities here, not one . . .
there is the closed or condensed and the open or light, which
has to do with sweet things, dreams, fun, reveries, desires . . .
they are all something opening, they don't belong to the world

of differences. If you know a depressing thought, you cannot make any deductions about fluffy thoughts for that person . . .

B: I have to interrupt you. This word 'fluffy' is crazy. No one could take that seriously. I think you should use something more like 'providential' as we have used it before, implying a sense of possibility or richness. 'Fluffy' sounds like a pet dog . . .

A: Very droll . . . Help me find a better word then . . . You must have some sense of what I am trying to say.

B: Yes, there is a sense of lightness, flow . . . possibility . . . reverie . . . imagination, and it does seem a separate dimension . . . but there is also the sense of depth in this . . . we talked before of positive depth . . . It is not just sweetness . . . sometimes it can be painful but feel somehow healing or moving, in a way . . . Let me give a personal example. About a year ago, I was discussing some experiences of mine from my late teenage years. They were not things I thought of often, but they were quite painful and I had always looked back on them with some sense of shame and inadequacy. It was unusual in that the person I was speaking to had been through quite similar circumstances. What I realized in talking to him about these experiences which I had always felt badly about, was that I had actually been quite used. When I connected with this, I felt a mix of anger, pain, betrayal and relief. All that time I had carried some weight of these things and in that moment of conversation that changed quite markedly. But the change wasn't light or sweet in the sense you imply. It was like a different sort of pain which felt more real, more true, somehow deeper but very freeing . . .

A: Yes, lightness is only one part . . . but even with what you just described you seemed lighter . . . you implied that you stopped carrying a weight.

B: Could we again use 'poetic' for what we mean – it is not perfect, but when people read poetry they expect to associate to feelings beyond the words – the poetic world is distinct from the referential world . . . In a poetic world people expect laughter, or the ethereal, or poignancy. Another word which might describe it is 'imaginist'. It's a bit obscure, apparently it was introduced by Jane Austen, it means 'a person of active imaginaton and speculative temper' according to my dictionary. I was looking at the various assocations of 'imagine' and noticed this.

A: An 'imaginist perspective' . . . 'imaginism' . . . it has a certain ring to it.

B: Yes, it does . . . maybe we should forget the 'multiplicity' and 'providence' we've been talking about and concentrate on imaginism . . . it sounds very marketable . . . a good product . . . By the way, the one metaphor everyone avoids is therapy as product.

A: (*laughs*) . . . We agonize for years over getting the right description and then we'll be trapped by it. Perhaps we should never agree on a best word. So . . . let me recap: this understanding . . . 'poetic' or 'imaginist' we are proposing has to do with multiple realities, potentialities, multivocality. It has links with poems, dreams, myths, meditation and art. It is a kind of upward drift, a dimension of openness in everything. It cannot be in a specific place, it only exists in relationships, as their potentials.

B: Not a bad condensation. It kind of associates with many things we have talked about . . . but it still sounds a little strange.

A: And I really do think that what helps people belongs to this sphere. Things which are really helpful do not come from the reality of logical arguments. They cannot be forced to come to us – but we can open ourselves to them. These things are more about submission, in a sense.

B: In what sense?

A: In the sense we have talked about many times. I think we are to a great extent talking of the relaxation of the need to prove something is right and something is wrong. Opening to the emotions, to the spirits of the moments. And here, I think, identity logic is a major villain. Conflicts destroy the poetic. Being right destroys the sense of open possibility. Moral high ground destroys it. And I think research, at least non-participatory research, mostly does the same. So we have lots of problems ahead.

B: Why?

A: Because the whole Western world is founded on the identity logic. But I am optimistic in a way. Nobody or nothing can ever succeed in killing the providential context of interaction Bakhtin is talking about. It is recreated in every dialogue. Attempts to know everything or control interaction make themselves ridiculous in the end.

B: But that end can be a long time from here. But let's not get into that. There seems to be a religious dimension there somewhere . . . do I hear you right?

A: I agree. But I don't mean any specific religion, I mean a sense of sacredness. Because all of this has to do with multivocality. And sacredness has to do with multiple realities . . .

A: But research . . . can it not produce multivocality in any sense? I think it can. It can.

B: In the sense that it can help in maintaining more varied discussions in society. If we had only the businessmen or politicians' voices . . . what a horrible idea. Compare it to the type of experiences and joys produced by children's tales, good conversations, enjoying good wine . . .

A: Is there a hint there?

B: Yes . . . You can tell these things.

A: Red or white?

B: Red, please.

B: I'll get some. We can have it on the verandah.

(*A long silence, sounds of crickets.*)

B: You know I would like to see *Red*, the movie. Maybe we could see it tonight. It is just ten to five.

A: Why not.

B: . . . You know, I was just thinking of that story of Borges that says 'the poetry of the Urns consists of a single word'. There seems so much more to say but I seem not to have more words. Sometimes there seems too many of them. But first, I have to clean up a little and get dinner ready. You can help. Otherwise, you might get too much lightness and float away.

A: I agree, let's start the opsological phase.

B: What?

A: Opsology is Greek. It refers to the art of cookery, art of dinners. Dinner is a nice metaphor for a common providential project.

7

Attempts at Closure

Closure 1: The last café

A: Ohh . . . What is he doing? . . . I really hate those drivers who drive close behind you. There was a bumper sticker I saw on a car a couple of days ago. It said 'If you can read this, I'll slam my brakes on'.

(*A long silence.*)

A: Why are you so silent? . . .

B: . . . Yes I am quite silent . . . I am out of words again.

A: Do you feel OK going back? What time does your plane leave?

B: 12:30.

A: Could you close the window a bit, I can't hear anything?

B: Is it better now? I guess it feels OK to go back, there are things to look forward to. It is just that I feel a little flat. . . . I'll check once more . . . yes, the plane leaves half past twelve. So, we have still some time. It would be nice to continue these discussions. There are not too many people back home to talk to about the things we are talking about. That feels quite hopeless sometimes. We could stop to have coffee at that shop over there . . . we have a couple of extra minutes.

A: Yes . . .

(. . .)

A: This coffee is quite stale. So, where were we? I am quite lonely here too.

B: Are you?

A: So where is the hope?

B: Where is the hope?

A: Where is the hope . . . do you know where it is? Is there hope anywhere?

B: You sound so bleak . . . I think some of it is in the cafés . . . here and in my town . . . and also at dinner tables. And if I go to cafés alone, I will remember our discussions.

A: The same with me. And I remember our friendship . . . it has its home in cafés.

B: (*half-singing*) Give me a home where the cappuccino foam . . .

A: You know . . . I have been thinking more of the research stuff. I am not that pessimistic any more.

B: So what happened?

A: I think there could be ways to do research on what is useful in conversations. The idea came to my head when we talked about that young woman and the poetic sensibility. I think it would make sense to just study the production of good moments, sparkling moments in therapy.

B: How? And how about the generalization? And how to choose the clients and sessions?

A: Are you my friend or are you not? We could just tape the sessions and do a couple of things. We could see what precedes sparkling moments or enjoyable moments.

B: So, what about the generalization of these good moments? Maybe they are absolutely meaningless regarding what happens outside the therapy?

A: But if we see the therapy as good or constructive dialogue and if we can show that the experience of participating in constructive dialogue correlates positively with good results measured in other ways. Aren't we then quite far? And there is already some research which confirms this connection.

B: I can live with that.

A: So, the task would be to show that when we can produce this kind of good interaction, we are in fact doing good therapy. If we could show this, we could then perhaps also show that what makes for good therapy might really come quite close to what makes for any good conversation.

B: Another question. Do you think what we are saying can distinguish between existing methods of therapy? Are they all as good . . . or as bad? I think it can.

A: I think we can . . . if we can make a distinction between good and bad interaction . . . or between good and bad times . . . or being treated well or badly. What disturbs me a little is that this way of thinking bypasses the dilemma of the importance of challenges and things like that.

B: Do you see any bad news in what we say?

A: I am not sure. The bad news might be that from some perspectives it seems that at least some of the methods of the shared search of promise must be built together again and again. On the other hand, all kinds of standard procedures of professionals can feel unique to clients. Think of car dealers and their customers, or of the standard home assignments which are still used by some family therapists, or even of the unique reactions to absolutely standard placebo pills. So, the question of what is really hand-made and who makes hand-made hand-made is quite difficult in this connection. But I think that people naturally have a good nose for deadness in interaction. Maybe there is so much aliveness in people that it can be enhanced even by dead interaction.

B: I'll accept that as a reasonably good point. It is acceptable. Yes . . .

A: So, it's time . . . Do you have everything – passport, money . . . your head and soul?

B: Yes, I have everything.

A: Hug?

B: (*smiles*)

   (*Hugging*)

A: OK . . . Well . . . I'll call you. We will meet. I'll send you the next draft by E-mail . . . in a couple of weeks.

B: OK.

A: Should we go?

B: I guess so . . .

Closure 2: Dionysian remarks

Is there a place for a summary or condensation in a book like this? Perhaps, perhaps not.

What is the method we are proposing? Are we proposing a method? Yes we are, in a way. The best description of this method is perhaps that the therapists should be serious and playful at the same time. They should have their tongue in their cheek and have a straight face at the same time. They should listen to signs of promise. There should be play, there should be trust, there should be willingness to see real injustices.

To have a psychological problem is to be alone and powerless – at times. It is to be a prisoner of one reality, one fate, one language, one emotion, one description – at times.

So, are we talking about relationships, thoughts or emotions – or about words? Sincerely, we don't think that words, emotions, thoughts and relationships can be separated. They come together. There are deadly and depressing ways of talking, thinking and relating. They have to be dialogized. This can happen in therapy. It can also happen without therapy. Often it can happen by changing a relationship – and different words, new or forgotten ones, will follow. The new words can also be followed by different thoughts, experience and relationships. The order does not really matter. What we have is a loop of words, thoughts, experience and relationships.

The methods of therapy? Many methods of therapy can be helpful. We believe that the more contact they allow with enlivening ideas, relationships, experiences and words, and the more they can do this in the spirit of trust, the better they work. Some methods of therapy contain very useful guidelines and principles: they encourage talk which easily invites shared signs of promise and allows this to happen in a client-driven way. They help many voices to be found which had been silenced before.

How to be playful and poetic? How to do that in the spirit of trust? We see this as both an emotional and literary task. Alive talk, enlivening talk stems from being alive. Trust requires seeing and acknowledging the pain of others and ourselves, and attempting to repair the breaches in relationships.

Being alive requires respect for Dionysian, earthly values – emotions, pleasures, play, connectedness. This requires distancing oneself from the academic stances typical of more objectivistic approaches to helping. This is not necessarily as difficult as it seems. The world seems to be moving in that direction anyway. The belief in cold, detached reason is being left behind.

Closure 3: Therapy as the art of good interaction

In the preceding text we have focused on resources that help people to go on successfully with their lives and with each other. We hope we have succeeded in showing that the same resources are also used in successful therapy. Our main interest has involved (i) the ambiguity of meanings of words, interaction, social positions and experience and (ii) realms of sociality. We have also talked about the connections of the domain of sacredness and the element of discursive variation (freshness, surprise) to ambiguity and sociality.

On these last pages we will make an attempt to bring some of the discussions about these topics together. But first some reminders of the views of therapy which we have presented so far.

We see therapy as a continuous development and reshaping of shared, providential realities. These realities are not attributes of individuals. They are rather something *in* which the persons themselves are, and *to* which they act and react. They are dialogical phenomena produced together by the participants. Yet they cannot be totally controlled by them. Joint action is more than a sum of its individual parts (see Shotter, 1993a).

Concepts like 'providential dialogue', 'providential context' and 'providential interaction' are easily understandable from the perspective of everyday life. They refer to practices which are in use when people treat each other and themselves well. This form of everyday action and knowledge stands in contrast to those professional approaches which

presumptions, prepositions, set aside

see people either as the targets of their (well-meaning) operations of cure or education, or as consumers who choose between receiving services designed by the experts.

The dialogical approach we are proposing starts from the premiss that both helpful and problematic realities ('solutions' and 'problems') are examples of joint action in Shotter's sense. An implication of this view is that all participants have responsibilities in the co-creation of helpful contexts. All of them thus also deserve credit for success. The sad thing is that many of our actual practices of therapy seem to decrease the visibility of everyday knowledges needed in the creation of providential forms of interaction.

What do we mean by seeing ambiguity and sociality as basic resources? In regard to ambiguity, we can remind ourselves of Bakhtin's concept 'heteroglossia' and of many deconstructionist notions of meaning. Bakhtin tells us that all talk, writing and behaviour is born in a field of tension of centripetal and centrifugal forces. The former are forces of standardization of meanings, the latter have to do with the undeniable uniqueness of each speech situation. In Bakhtin's view each utterance is both a creative occurrence *and* a product of foreign and normative forces.

Milan Kundera has in his book *The Art of the Novel* presented a rather similar point in a different way. For him each novel poses the question: 'From what does the enchantment of human life come?' Many novelists, Kundera among them, are claiming that the mystery and poetry comes from the stopping of action, from contemplative moments, from leaving the world of causes and effects, from ambiguity and unpredictability. Poetry is *sine ratione*. It is born where the action collapses, where the bridge between cause and effect breaks down, where the thought wanders in sweet freedom. But can this view ever fit the activist and productivist worlds of therapy or health and social care?

We have tried to show quite extensively in our discussions how important it is to develop more relational and discursive views of therapy. It is evident that individualist and objectivistic notions of problems, solutions and therapeutic interaction are too limited and limiting. Their use prevents seeing resources linked to language and dialogues and also to clients' families, friends and colleagues. They also make it difficult to see how possibilities and connectedness are produced and lost in everyday life.

It seems obvious that the dimension of sacredness, linked to the ambiguity of realities and to the sense of depth and mystery, is crucially important for human flourishing. This domain does not belong only to religions. Following Shotter and Bakhtin we can see a sense of sacred as an (often obscured) dimension of all dialogue and joint action. It is an experience of a relationship to something bigger than individual selves and intentions. Because a sense of the sacred is an antidote to one-dimensionality and machine-likeness, it has a close connection both to a sense of available options and to the experience of personal worth and dignity.

The discursive creation of providence and personal worth relates also to the possibility of thematic variation and interactional freshness. When we study any group of people in informal conversations, we see that they jump relentlessly from topic to topic, from one point of view to another. The old topics and perspectives often become stale quite quickly and something which refreshens the minds of participants is needed. Discursive situations are problematic when any participants are denied the right to thematic variation and surprising changes of perspectives. These situations can sometimes produce a sense of safety and predictability. They can, however, also easily be experienced as painful and dehumanizing. Freshness in this sense seems to be a basic social resource with which people can keep conversations interesting and morally regrading to *all* participants.

To give a taste of the ways of connecting ambiguity, the social and sacredness we will return again briefly to the work of Michael Maffesoli, who has written extensively about aesthetic and social forms of rationality. Maffesoli claims that certain forms of historically earlier types of sociality are actually breaking through the more mechanical forms, typical of the modern stages of societies. What we see, he says, is that people organize their interaction and lives more and more around things, hobbies, interests on affective and aesthetic, rather than rational bases. The aesthetic–hedonistic, Dionysian rationality is vastly different from the rationality of production. It is to a great extent 'confusional'. People want to be a part of something, to merge with something, to forget clear borders and definitions, to forget their individual identities, to submerge in something which surpasses their personal limits. Maffesoli conceptualizes this type of sociality as a subterranean force connecting people. He sees this power as the invisible centre of life, as the source of will to aliveness. Individual experiences of meaningfulness can also be linked to it.

Similar phenomena have also been described by other writers. Kenneth Gergen has recently referred to something resembling the Dionysian orientation with the concept of 'relational sublime' (Gergen, 1994). We can add the concept of 'sacredness'.

We could say that a basic criterion for providential interaction is that all participants find it satisfactory and meaningful. It encourages and invites – in fact requires – all participants to use their skills to create connectedness, meaningfulness and promise together.

After saying all this it is perhaps possible to see that the project we are suggesting is really not limited to therapy. It could rather be seen as an attempt to seek conceptual resources for supporting more providential forms of interaction (or forms of interaction which are genuinely worthy of a human being) in many spheres of life. We are convinced that developing our understanding about inter-relationships of ambiguity, sociality and sacredness helps us not only to develop more respectful clinical practices, but to combine questions of therapy to questions discussed in realms like arts, literature and religion.

Should we be pessimistic or optimistic regarding the project? If we start from the views proposed by Vico, Bakhtin and Shotter and see providentiality as an essential feature of dialogical interaction, we can see good grounds for being optimistic. Attempts to obscure options, possibilities and multivocality bring to mind the children's tale of 'The Emperor's New Clothes' – it seems that there is something deeply *illusory* in the experienced lack of providentiality. On the other hand, looking at many practices in working life, academic writing and helping shows that enlivening potentials of interaction are easily denied, lost and overlooked.

The resources of language *combined* with both the motive and the shared responsibility for creating good interaction will, together, create infinite potentials for providential interaction. Difficulties in seeing and using these potentials relate to problems in creating trust and connectedness and difficulties in utilizing the inherent exuberance, providence and verdancy of all interaction.

At this point we can look to the swarming possibilities of the future. What we see is a series of new beginnings: a multiplicity not just of models and theories but also of passions, connections and inspirations. We can see conversations becoming more alive, infused with both the playful and the sacred. We can see more and more readiness to move from topic to topic to discover shared places in which we can find joy or dignity together. We can see it becoming easier and easier to celebrate the discontinuities and ambiguities which academic disciplines usually try to erase. And we can look to learn more and more about how to use the plays of light and shadow as doorways to new possibilities.

References

Allende, I. (1991) *The Stories of Eva Luna*. Penguin, London.

Anderson, H. and Goolishian, H. (1988) A view of human systems as linguistic systems: preliminary and evolving ideas about the implications for clinical theory, *Family Process*, 27: 371–393.

Bachelard G. (1994) *The Poetics of Space*. Beacon Press, Boston, MA.

Bakhtin, M. (1981) *The Dialogic Imagination: Four Essays by M.M. Bakhtin* (ed. M. Holquist). University of Texas Press, Austin.

Bakhtin, M. (1986) *Speech Genres and Other Late Essays* (tr. Vern W. McGee). University of Texas Press, Austin.

Barthes, R. (1975) *The Pleasure of the Text*. Hill and Wang, New York.

Barthes, R. (1993a) Excerpt from *The Pleasure of the Text*. In S. Sontag (ed.), *A Roland Barthes Reader* (pp. 404–414). Vintage, London.

Barthes, R. (1993b) Roland Barthes by Roland Barthes. In S. Sontag (ed.), *A Roland Barthes Reader* (pp. 415–425). Vintage, London.

Bartlett, F. (1932) *Remembering: A Study in Experimental Psychology*. Cambridge University Press, London.

Billig, M. (1987) *Arguing and Thinking: A Rhetorical Approach to Social Psychology*. Cambridge University Press, Cambridge.

Billig, M. (1991) *Ideology and Opinions: Studies in Rhetorical Psychology*. Sage, London.

Bruner, J. (1986) *Actual Minds, Possible Worlds*. Harvard University Press, Cambridge, MA.

Bruner, J. (1987) Life as a narrative, *Social Research*, 54: 11–32.

Bruner, J. (1990) *Acts of Meaning*. Harvard University Press, Cambridge, MA.

De Shazer, S. (1985) *Keys to Solutions in Brief Therapy*. W.W. Norton, New York.

De Shazer, S. (1988) *Clues to Investigation of Solutions in Brief Therapy*. W.W. Norton, New York.

De Shazer, S. (1991) *Putting Difference to Work*. W.W. Norton, New York.

De Shazer, S. (1994) *Words Were Originally Magic*. W.W. Norton, New York.

Eliade, M. (1991) *Myth of the Eternal Return: Or Cosmos and History*. Princeton University Press, Princeton, NJ.

Epston, D. (1989) Workshop presentation. Dulwich Centre, Adelaide.

Fuentes, C. (1995) Accidents of time. In N.T. Di Giovanni (ed.), *The Borges Tradition*. Constable, London.

Furman, B. and Ahola, T. (1992) *Solution Talk – Hosting Therapeutic Conversations*. W.W. Norton, New York.

176   *Re-imagining therapy*

Garfinkel, H. (1967) *Studies in Ethnomethodology.* Prentice-Hall, Englewood Cliffs, NJ.

Gergen, K. (1994) *Realities and Relationships: Soundings in Social Constructionism.* Harvard University Press, Cambridge, MA/London.

Goffman, E. (1959) *The Presentation of Self in Everyday Life.* Doubleday, New York.

Haley, J. (1973) *Uncommon Therapy: The Psychiatric Techniques of Milton H. Erickson.* W.W. Norton, New York.

Hall, R. (1994) Partnership and accountability, *Dulwich Centre Newsletter*, 2 and 3: 6–28.

Harland, R. (1987) *Superstructuralism: The Philosophy of Structuralism and Post-structuralism.* Methuen, London.

Harré, R. (1983) *Personal Being: A Theory for Individual Psychology.* Basil Blackwell, Oxford.

Hoffman, L. (1990) Constructing realities: an art of lenses, *Family Process*, 29: 1–12.

Hoffman, L. (1991) A reflexive stance for family therapy, *Journal of Strategic and Systemic Therapies*, 10: 4–17.

James, W. (1884) What is an emotion?, *Mind*, 9: 188–205.

Johnson, M. (1993) *Moral Imagination: Implications of Cognitive Science for Ethics.* University of Chicago Press, Chicago.

Lakoff, G. and Johnson, M. (1980) *Metaphors We Live By.* University of Chicago Press, Chicago.

Leskinen, J. (1994) *Äeti.* Kirjayhtymä OY, Helsinki.

Lutz, C. (1987) Goals, events and understanding in Infaluk emotion theory. In D. Holland and N. Quinn (eds), *Cultural Models in Language and Thought.* Cambridge University Press, Cambridge.

MacIntyre, A. (1981) *After Virtue.* Duckworth, London.

Maffesoli, M. (1993) *The Shadow of Dionysus: A Contribution to the Sociology of the Orgy.* State University of New York Press, Albany.

Makkonen, M. (1994) From machine analogies to human analogies – examining the methods of gigolos and therapists. A presentation in the Second Dialogical Forum, November 26–27, Helsinki.

Middleton, D. and Edwards, D. (1990) *Collective Remembering.* Sage, London.

Morson, G. and Emerson, C. (1990) *Mikhail Bakhtin: Creation of Prosaics.* Stanford University Press, Stanford, CA.

Norris, C. (1983) *The Deconstructive Turn.* Methuen, New York.

Norris, C. (1987) *Derrida.* Fontana Press, London.

O'Hanlon, W. and Weiner-Davis, M. (1989) *In Search of Solutions: A New Direction in Psychotherapy.* W.W. Norton, New York.

Penman, R. (1992) Good theory and good practice: an argument in progress, *Communication Theory*, 2(3): 234–250.

Queneau, R. (1981) *Exercises in Style.* New Directions Books, New York.

Riikonen, E. (1992) Auttamistyön ongelmakäsitykset ja haastattelukäytännöt. Ongelmakielestä kompetenssikieleen (Problem models and interviewing practices in professional helping: From problem-focused language to competence-focused language), Kuntoutussäätiön tutkimuksia 32/1992, Doctoral dissertation in psychiatry, University of Oulu.

Riikonen, E. and Mattila, A. (1994) Ovatko psykiatriset ongelmamallit ja luokitukset masentavia? (Are psychiatric problem models and classification systems depressing?) *Duodecim*, 3: 347–359.

Rosaldo, M. (1984) Towards an anthropology of self and feeling. In R. Shweder and R. LeVine, *Culture Theory: Essays on Mind, Self and Emotion.* Cambridge University Press, Cambridge.

Rossi, E. (1986) *The Psychobiology of Mind–Body Healing.* W.W. Norton, New York.

Serres, M. (1993) *La Légende des Anges.* Flammarion, Paris.

Shotter, J. (1993a) *Cultural Politics of Everyday Life: Social Constructionism, Rhetoric and Knowing of the Third Kind.* Open University Press, Buckingham.

Shotter, J. (1993b) *Conversational Realities.* Sage, London.

Simonov, P.V. (1970) The information theory of emotion. In M.B. Arnold (ed.), *Feelings and Emotions: The Loyola Symposium.* Academic Press, New York.

Smith, G. (1988) Fighting fighting: a struggle to overcome violence, *Family Therapy Case Studies*, 3(2): 17–25.

Smith, G. (1992a) Metaphoric therapy: exploring the pervasiveness of metaphor and its use in therapy, *Australian and New Zealand Journal of Family Therapy*, 13: 272–278.

Smith, G. (1992b) Dichotomies in the making of men, *Dulwich Centre Newsletter*, 3 and 4: 9–23.

Tamasese, K. and Waldegrave, C. (1993) Cultural and gender accountability in the 'Just Therapy' approach, *Journal of Feminist Family Therapy*, 5(2): 29–45.

Taylor, C. (1989) *Sources of Self: The Making of Modern Identity.* Cambridge University Press, Cambridge.

Vygotsky, L. (1986) *Thought and Language.* MIT Press, Cambridge, MA.

Waldegrave, C. (1990) Just therapy. *Dulwich Centre Newsletter*, 1: 5–46.

Wertsch, J. (1991) *Voices of the Mind.* Harvester Wheatsheaf, Hemel Hempstead.

White, G. (1990) Moral discourse and the rhetoric of emotions. In C. Lutz and L. Abu-Lughod (eds), *Language and the Politics of Emotion.* Cambridge University Press, Cambridge.

White, M. (1989) *Selected Papers.* Dulwich Centre Publications, Adelaide.

White, M. (1991) Deconstruction and therapy. *Dulwich Centre Newsletter*, 2.

White, M. (1995) *Re-authoring Lives.* Dulwich Centre Publications, Adelaide.

White, M. and Epston, D. (1990) *Narrative Means to Therapeutic Ends.* W.W. Norton, New York.

Wittgenstein, L. (1953) *Philosophical Investigations.* Basil Blackwell, Oxford.

Index